OPPOSING VIEWPOINTS® SERIES

Smartphones

Other Books of Related Interest:

"Congress shall make
no law . . . abridging
the freedom of speech,
or of the press."

First Amendment to the US Constitution

The basic foundation of our democracy is the First Amendment guarantee of freedom of expression. The Opposing Viewpoints series is dedicated to the concept of this basic freedom and the idea that it is more important to practice it than to enshrine it.

Smartphones

Roman Espejo, Book Editor

GREENHAVEN PRESS
A part of Gale, Cengage Learning

GALE
CENGAGE Learning

Detroit • New York • San Francisco • New Haven, Conn • Waterville, Maine • London

Elizabeth Des Chenes, *Director, Publishing Solutions*

© 2013 Greenhaven Press, a part of Gale, Cengage Learning.

Gale and Greenhaven Press are registered trademarks used herein under license.

For more information, contact:
Greenhaven Press
27500 Drake Rd.
Farmington Hills, MI 48331-3535
Or you can visit our Internet site at gale.cengage.com

For product information and technology assistance, contact us at

Gale Customer Support, 1-800-877-4253
For permission to use material from this text or product, submit all requests online at
www.cengage.com/permissions

Further permissions questions can be emailed to permissionrequest@cengage.com

Articles in Greenhaven Press anthologies are often edited for length to meet page requirements. In addition, original titles of these works are changed to clearly present the main thesis and to explicitly indicate the author's opinion. Every effort is made to ensure that Greenhaven Press accurately reflects the original intent of the authors. Every effort has been made to trace the owners of copyrighted material.

Cover Image copyright © Flydragon/Shutterstock.com.

LIBRARY OF CONGRESS CATALOGING-IN-PUBLICATION DATA

Smartphones / Roman Espejo, book editor.
    p. cm. -- (Opposing viewpoints)
    Summary: "Opposing Viewpoints: Smartphones: Opposing Viewpoints is the leading source for libraries and classrooms in need of current-issue materials. The viewpoints are selected from a wide range of highly respected sources and publications"-- Provided by publisher.
    Includes bibliographical references and index.
    ISBN 978-0-7377-6342-3 (hardback) -- ISBN 978-0-7377-6343-0 (paperback)
    1. Mobile computing. 2. Smartphones--Social aspects. 3. Pocket computers--Social aspects. I. Espejo, Roman, 1977- editor of compilation.
    QA76.59.S59 2013
    004.167--dc23
                                        2012040794

Printed in the United States of America
1 2 3 4 5   17 16 15 14 13

Contents

Chapter 3: Do Smartphones Have Privacy Risks?

Chapter 4: What Is the Future of Smartphones?

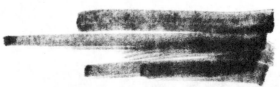

Why Consider Opposing Viewpoints?

> "The only way in which a human being can make some approach to knowing the whole of a subject is by hearing what can be said about it by persons of every variety of opinion and studying all modes in which it can be looked at by every character of mind. No wise man ever acquired his wisdom in any mode but this."
>
> *John Stuart Mill*

In our media-intensive culture it is not difficult to find differing opinions. Thousands of newspapers and magazines and dozens of radio and television talk shows resound with differing points of view. The difficulty lies in deciding which opinion to agree with and which "experts" seem the most credible. The more inundated we become with differing opinions and claims, the more essential it is to hone critical reading and thinking skills to evaluate these ideas. Opposing Viewpoints books address this problem directly by presenting stimulating debates that can be used to enhance and teach these skills. The varied opinions contained in each book examine many different aspects of a single issue. While examining these conveniently edited opposing views, readers can develop critical thinking skills such as the ability to compare and contrast authors' credibility, facts, argumentation styles, use of persuasive techniques, and other stylistic tools. In short, the Opposing Viewpoints Series is an ideal way to attain the higher-level thinking and reading skills so essential in a culture of diverse and contradictory opinions.

In addition to providing a tool for critical thinking, Opposing Viewpoints books challenge readers to question their own strongly held opinions and assumptions. Most people form their opinions on the basis of upbringing, peer pressure, and personal, cultural, or professional bias. By reading carefully balanced opposing views, readers must directly confront new ideas as well as the opinions of those with whom they disagree. This is not to argue simplistically that everyone who reads opposing views will—or should—change his or her opinion. Instead, the series enhances readers' understanding of their own views by encouraging confrontation with opposing ideas. Careful examination of others' views can lead to the readers' understanding of the logical inconsistencies in their own opinions, perspective on why they hold an opinion, and the consideration of the possibility that their opinion requires further evaluation.

Evaluating Other Opinions

To ensure that this type of examination occurs, Opposing Viewpoints books present all types of opinions. Prominent spokespeople on different sides of each issue as well as well-known professionals from many disciplines challenge the reader. An additional goal of the series is to provide a forum for other, less known, or even unpopular viewpoints. The opinion of an ordinary person who has had to make the decision to cut off life support from a terminally ill relative, for example, may be just as valuable and provide just as much insight as a medical ethicist's professional opinion. The editors have two additional purposes in including these less known views. One, the editors encourage readers to respect others' opinions—even when not enhanced by professional credibility. It is only by reading or listening to and objectively evaluating others' ideas that one can determine whether they are worthy of consideration. Two, the inclusion of such viewpoints encourages the important critical thinking skill of objectively evaluating an author's credentials and bias. This evaluation will illuminate an author's reasons for taking a particular stance on an issue and will aid in readers' evaluation of the author's ideas.

It is our hope that these books will give readers a deeper understanding of the issues debated and an appreciation of the complexity of even seemingly simple issues when good and honest people disagree. This awareness is particularly important in a democratic society such as ours in which people enter into public debate to determine the common good. Those with whom one disagrees should not be regarded as enemies but rather as people whose views deserve careful examination and may shed light on one's own.

Thomas Jefferson once said that "difference of opinion leads to inquiry, and inquiry to truth." Jefferson, a broadly educated man, argued that "if a nation expects to be ignorant and free . . . it expects what never was and never will be." As individuals and as a nation, it is imperative that we consider the opinions of others and examine them with skill and discernment. The Opposing Viewpoints series is intended to help readers achieve this goal.

David L. Bender and Bruno Leone,
Founders

Introduction

"Smartphones offer significant benefits for the more than 1 billion people who live with some form of disability."

—Vodaphone Group,
*"The Smartphone Revolution:
Accessible to All," December 6, 2011*

"Smartphone apps are changing how millions of people manage their daily lives, but some groups in society risk missing out on the smartphone revolution."

—Andrew Dunnett,
director of the Vodafone Foundation

In October 2010, President Barack Obama signed a bill aiming to ease the use of technologies for the deaf and blind. "The 21st Century Communications and Video Accessibility Act will make it easier for people who are deaf, blind, or live with a visual impairment to do what many of us take for granted—from navigating a TV or DVD menu to sending an e-mail on a smartphone," Obama declared at the signing of the bill. For smartphones, the federal guidelines created by the law call for the improvement of interfaces to make accessing the Internet easier. "It sets new standards so that Americans with disabilities can take advantage of the technology our economy depends on," Obama added.

In fact with the boom of mobile technology over the past decade, disabled individuals are adopting smartphones in their daily lives. For example, according to a May 2012 article in the *New York Times*, Richard Einhorn uses his in busy restaurants and crowded places, where he has a hard time listening to voices with his hearing aid. Using an application that processes and boosts sound on his iPhone, he plugs an omnidirectional microphone into it and puts on earphones. "I put the iPhone on the table," says Einhorn, a composer who suffered significant hearing loss in 2010. "I point it at whoever's talking, and I can have conversations with them. Soon we forget the iPhone is sitting there." His setup is an effective solution, according to Jay T. Rubinstein, a professor of bioengineering and otolaryngology at the University of Washington. "It makes sense when you need to capture a speaker's voice in a noisy environment," Rubinstein observes in the *New York Times* article. "A system that gives you a high-quality directional mike and good earphones can help people hear in a complex setting."

Individuals with disabilities are also designing smartphone applications based on their own experiences and obstacles. T.V. Raman, a blind Google researcher, helped develop an app for the Android operating system to help the visually impaired. After the shuttle bus he takes home unexpectedly dropped him off on the opposite side of the street, Raman and his colleagues were inspired to create an app that utilizes the global positioning system (GPS) and audio capabilities of a smartphone to help the user navigate his or her surroundings. "Now when you touch the phone, it tells you which way you're pointing and where you are," Raman states in a 2009 *Globe and Mail* article. "The fact that you're blind is your own business. The computer doesn't need to know that." Also, David Biddle, who lost his legs, one eye, and part of his spleen in the July 2005 London terrorist attacks, created an app for those who require wheelchair or other assistance in the city. "I can think of numerous instances where I've stopped somewhere to use the toilet or gone to a restaurant only to find it is impossible. There is such a lack of useful information for people in a wheelchair, those with learning difficulties, or people with a visual or hearing impairment," he asserts in a January 2012 interview with BBC News. In collaboration with his friend Tobi Collett, Biddle released Ldn Access, which locates ramps as well as restrooms, parking, and other facilities with services for the disabled. The location-based app also provides information on attractions, entertainment, and hotels that are accessible for those with disabilities. "With this app we hope to use the latest technology to change people's mindsets and show how the disability isn't the problem, the lack of access is the problem," Biddle contends.

However, many observers still view smartphones as a challenge to use for disabled individuals, and some critics suggest that disabled individuals as a group are largely overlooked by designers and developers. "The iPhone provided some accessibility options but it felt like a bit of an afterthought," insists Geoff McCormick, director of design consultancy TheAlloy, in an interview with the *Guardian* in 2011. "The average phone designer is a male, in his 20s, so a great deal more empathy is required to understand the challenges of a 60-year-old man or a disabled mother of two," he points out. The smartphone interface, for instance, is a problem for Hee-young Kim; due to his impaired vision, the full potential of various functions and apps is lost to him. In an interview in the *Korea Times*, Kim claims, "It appears that social discrimination against the disabled has perished to a great extent." Kim, who lives in South Korea—home to Samsung, the world's largest cell phone manufacturer—continues, "But smartphones may be one of the last obstacles hindering the disabled like me."

The innovations and frustrations smartphones bring to people with disabilities underline some of the issues that users of the technology face. *Opposing Viewpoints: Smartphones* explores such areas of debate—from user friendliness to the devices as a primary means of going online—in the following chapters: What Are the Benefits of Smartphones?, Who Owns and Uses Smartphones?, Do Smartphones Have Privacy Risks?, and What Is the Future of Smartphones? The views, opinions, and analyses selected for this volume investigate the possibilities and limitations of mobile technology now and in the future.

OPPOSING
VIEWPOINTS®
SERIES

CHAPTER 1

What Are the Benefits of Smartphones?

Chapter Preface

For the office assistant and executive alike, smartphones have transformed mobile computing. Software and functions once tied to the desktop computer—word processing, spreadsheet programs, alphanumeric keyboards—have been unleashed and built into a single handheld that can fit into a pocket. In addition, speedier data services, increased accessibility of wireless broadband, and video conferencing keep workers connected with smartphones at their fingertips.

According to the 2012 AT&T Small Business Technology Poll, 85 percent of small businesses have integrated the devices in their operations, and 50 percent report that surviving would be impossible or a major challenge without mobile applications. Employees even use their own—not company issued—smartphones to work. "It's not just executives or 'road warrior' workers who are connecting—a whole host of knowledge workers are using personal smartphones or other mobile devices to log into their e-mail and work applications for the convenience of it," Sarah Sorensen, principal of Sorensen Consulting, writes in a 2010 article for *Forbes*.

However, smartphones are also associated with blurring the separation between the office and home, increasing employee stress. A 2012 survey from business mobile service provider iPass found that 60 percent of mobile workers work between fifty and sixty hours a week, most commonly filling up daytime on weekends. Furthermore, 58 percent of North American workers, along with 55 percent of European workers and 71 percent of Asian workers, report sleeping with their devices. "Work invades the home far more than domestic chores invade the office," argues the *Economist* in a March 2012 article. "Otherwise-sane people check their smartphones obsessively, even during pre-dinner drinks, and send e-mails first thing in the morning and last thing at night." Other commentators express concern about the physical toll of overtime spent on smartphones. "While doing a bit of extra work at home may seem like a good short-term fix, if it becomes a regular part of your evening routine then it can lead to problems such as back and neck pain, as well as stress-related illness," maintains Helena Johnson, chair of the Chartered Society of Physiotherapy in the United Kingdom, in a June 2012 interview with BBC News. In the following chapter, the authors examine the touted advantages and disadvantages of smartphones.

> "It is beyond doubt that apps, and the new wave of phones in which they reside, are already influencing the way their users communicate with each other, navigate their environment and do business."

Smartphones Are Transforming Daily Life

Richard Fisher

Richard Fisher is a feature editor at the British magazine New Scientist. *In the following viewpoint, he proposes that smartphones and their apps are transforming everyday life. Fisher explains how he and other smartphone owners use them in wide-ranging situations and contexts, profoundly changing how people interact with the world, communicate, and process information. In fact, the devices are impacting cognitive processes and how memories and thoughts are retrieved, the author states. Also, because of their high level of personalization, contends Fisher, smartphones are drawing users away from traditional media and the Internet, and they will become the primary channel of information.*

As you read, consider the following questions:

1. In what situations does the author say he turns to smartphone apps?

2. What is Dean Eckles's view of app-enabled phones?

3. Why is Fisher concerned with how the iPhone affects people's decisions?

Friday 7:43 a.m.

My wife is standing at the door to the bathroom, watching me time my toothbrush routine using an application down-loaded to my iPhone. Thirty seconds on upper-right molars: done. "What are you doing?" she asks. "Nothing," I mumble through a mouthful of toothpaste. She doesn't speak, but her eyes say "I think I love you a little less." If only she under-stood.

Ever since I bought an Apple iPhone, I have been hooked on apps. Apple's App Store is a virtual shopping mall with all the shopaholic joy of a real mall but none of the annoying teenagers. It is packed to the virtual rafters with thousands of downloadable software tools. Admittedly, the store makes a bad first impression on many people, with novelty apps such as lightsabers dominating the top 25 chart. But dig a little deeper and you will find life-enhancing riches.

I confess that I now turn to the App Store in almost every situation. In unfamiliar places, I use apps to find the nearest gas station, cinema or even public toilet. I track the length and time of my commute. All my gym workouts are logged. Finding a nice place to eat while on the move is a cinch. Even this [viewpoint] is brought to you thanks to a voice recorder app (iDictaphone) that I used for recording interviews, and one that helped me "mind map" my thoughts when planning it out. Sometimes I daydream about becoming the most virtu-ally enhanced human in the world.

Thankfully, I am not the only one in this appy daze. I discovered that loads of people, including my colleagues, turn to their phones for help with all sorts of things. Up until a year ago, apps barely registered. Now these clever bits of software, when combined with the sensors and networking capabilities of today's smartphones, are sparking nothing short of a techno-cultural revolution. On the iPhone alone, Apple claims over 1.5 billion apps have been downloaded in just a year. The rest of the industry, including Nokia and Google, is now piling in with their own new or relaunched app stores.

Apps are more than just clever toys. While gaming still accounts for the lion's share of app activity, it is beyond doubt that apps, and the new wave of phones in which they reside, are already influencing the way their users communicate with each other, navigate their environment and do business. Arguably, these tailored bits of software—connected to the Internet, location-aware and sensor-supported as they are—may supersede the web. Some say the devices on which they reside are becoming a vital part of our selves, turning us into de facto cyborgs. Could these humble bits of code really have the potential to completely transform the way we interact with the world?

"Part Man, Part Computer"

Saturday 11:10 p.m.

Out with friends and last orders have been called in the pub. The alpha male of our group pulls out a stack of taxi numbers scrawled on old business cards. None of the firms is close enough. "Richard has a new iPhone—let's try that," my wife suggests. I pull up an app called AroundMe, which tells me where the nearest cab company is. Thirty seconds later and the taxi is on its way. My friends look on in envy and admiration. Alpha male looks despondent. "I am part man, part computer," I tell myself.

Some might ask what all the fuss is about. After all, downloadable applications appeared on some cell phones such as the Palm Treo almost a decade ago, so what's different now? The short answer is that the old apps were not particularly good. They were either difficult to download or time-consuming to master, so few people used them, says Gerard Goggin at the University of New South Wales in Sydney, Australia, who has studied the sociological impact of the iPhone.

Even people who think that Apple is all about glossy hype cannot deny that the iPhone changed things for everybody. Variously described as the Jesus phone, a concierge, a Swiss army knife or, somewhat disturbingly, a fingertip secretary, the iPhone is currently at the centre of the new app world. But forget the touch screen and sleek design, the truly revolutionary thing that Apple CEO [chief executive officer] Steve Jobs managed to do with the iPhone was to persuade cell phone network operators to loosen their grip on what phones could do. One of the consequences of this coup was the birth of the App Store, which Apple alone controlled and had designed to be as easy to browse as the iTunes Store.

What's more, Apple made it easy for anybody with some programming know-how to create an app: For $99 you can download the software development kit and gain intimate access to the phone's functions. Lured by the promise of riches, developers ranging from large software houses to bedroom enthusiasts have created a massive market of apps, virtually overnight.

An App for Any Occasion

Monday 7:25 p.m.

I have begun to track my cycle commute using an app called Trails, which records my path, altitude and speed as I travel. My aim is to find the fastest and shortest route to work. Today I achieved a new work-to-home record. "My god, what happened?" asked my wife as I shuffled through the

Smartphone Connectivity

Smartphones separate themselves in . . . [a] key area: connectivity. Many allow you to fetch e-mail from your corporate server or personal account, and several have QWERTY keypads that make replying from the road a real option. And instead of a plodding, text-only version of web surfing, smartphones have actual browsers that can render sites such as Google and Yahoo true to form.

Suzanne Kantra Kirschner,
"The PopSci Buyer's Guide: Smartphones,"
Popular Science, *vol. 266, no. 5, May 1, 2005.*

front door this evening. "You look terrible." I give her a self-satisfied grin. It was me versus the clock, and I won.

In the past year, many other companies have launched or re-branded their app stores for other handsets, including Nokia's Ovi Store and Google's Android marketplace. None has the sheer volume of the iPhone's store yet, but few technology analysts think Apple will remain the dominant purveyor of apps for long: Android offers significantly more freedom for developers than Apple, so could lure many of them away from the iPhone; Palm has been in the apps game for years; Research in Motion has the business market cornered with its BlackBerries; Nokia has legions of loyal European customers; and Microsoft is, well, Microsoft.

Even if these are not as successful as Apple's store, hundreds if not thousands of apps look likely to be available on most handsets. The explosion in investment coupled with the armies of developers means that there is already an app for almost any occasion. "The phone can take on many, many guises," says Goggin. "It can be a spirit level, a bowling ball, a budget balancer or a breathalyser." The device in your pocket is not a phone anymore. It is anything you want it to be.

A Huge Influence on Our Daily Behaviours

Saturday 4:30 p.m.

In a coffee shop casually flicking through the App Store. My finger hovers over an icon on the screen. Should I download MyVibe, a vibrator sex toy that was among the first X-rated apps Apple permitted? It feels so wrong, and yet . . .

The ability to use apps in almost any context raises the possibility that these devices could lead to profound changes in the way we navigate the world, communicate and absorb information. The app phenomenon is only a year old, but researchers are watching the surge closely. Many social scientists who study the influence of technology argue that app-enabled mobile devices are set to become a huge influence on our daily behaviours.

Sherry Turkle at Massachusetts Institute of Technology, who studies people's relationship with technology, says the power of the latest cell phones lies in the fact that they are "always on, always on you". With this capability, she says, the devices effectively become an appendage to our body and mind that plays a role in everything from our social interactions to emotions.

David Chalmers, a philosopher at the Australian National University in Canberra, agrees. He thinks cell phones are allowing cognition to creep beyond our skulls in entirely new ways. "Increasingly sophisticated information processing is being off-loaded to them," he says, so that smartphones are becoming a repository for our memory, desires and beliefs, and we can retrieve this information at will wherever we are. By aiding efficiency, navigation and local knowledge, apps achieve things that our biological brain alone could not.

An "Extension of Their Brains"

Sunday 2:30 p.m.

I'm visiting my parents. In the post-lunch lull I reach for my phone and am dismayed to find it isn't in my pocket. I feel like I've lost a limb. Fortunately my laptop is to hand. My mother peers over my shoulder. "It's a program called MobileMe," I explain. "I can use it to track my iPhone's location on a map if it's lost or stolen. No matter where it ends up in the world, I can see it."

"That's incredible!" she exclaims. "Anywhere in the world? So where is it now?"

"It's in my house," I reply relieved. You are off the hook this time, mother, I think, but I'm watching you.

The extra-appendage idea is backed up by a recent survey of the way people are using apps. Earlier this year [in 2009], a Chicago-based technology and design consultancy called Gravity Tank quizzed more than 1000 app users and conducted detailed interviews with a selection of them.

Over one-third of respondents said that they couldn't live without their app-loaded smartphones. "Apps are finding a meaningful place in people's daily diets," says Gravity Tank's Michael Winnick. "If you can access information and computing power anywhere and anytime, it'll impact on every part of human behaviour."

These people rely on apps to complete expense reports, monitor their pets remotely or manage their exercise regimes. Their smartphones have become a constantly evolving tool with the potential to instantly improve any moment, says Winnick. Some even reported that they perceived apps as an "extension of their brains".

In 10 to 15 years, app-enabled phones will be the number one channel through which we receive information, according to B.J. Fogg of Stanford University in Palo Alto, California, who studies the "persuasive" power of technologies. "We're building our lives around apps," he says. The devices know where we are and perhaps even what we are doing because of the phone's various sensors. Therefore, Fogg argues, they can provide highly personalised information that trumps the Internet, TV, radio or traditional media.

You can already see hints of this from the Gravity Tank survey: App users spend about 25 per cent less time reading newspapers, watching TV or using a computer since they started using apps.

Dean Eckles, also at Stanford, believes that app-enabled phones could become the sole "lens" through which we view the world. Our phones could soon influence our choices in day-to-day life without us even realizing it, he says. He bases his argument on studies showing that we are more likely to trust familiar technology that is physically near us. We develop a "quasi-social" relationship with it, he says.

An experiment by Youngme Moon, now at Harvard Business School, illustrates the point. It showed that people were more likely to provide personal information to a computer they had been sitting at for a while than another elsewhere in the room, even though they knew both were programmed in exactly the same way.

The cell phone is about as trusted and familiar to us as a gadget can be. No other technology is as close, so much of the time. It would be all too easy to put too much trust in apps, Eckles warns.

The Sole Lens Through Which We View the World

Friday 7:10 p.m.

Wandering through the streets of central London. Earlier, I checked an app called Yelp for restaurant tips. My wife and I have been walking towards the recommended venue for half an hour. I insist on ignoring all other establishments along the way. We lose mobile signal and become lost in the backstreets of Soho, just as it starts to rain. The look she gave me in the bathroom last Friday morning returns.

Plenty of apps, such as Yelp or AroundMe, help people discover what's in their vicinity, often filtered according to popularity or the reviews of other users. However, the quality and reliability of this ranking varies widely, says Eckles. One neighbourhood's recommendations are not always as robust as the next. The problem is that we could forget to think too deeply about this because we trust our phones implicitly. So it could become the case that if an app doesn't tell you there is a restaurant around the corner, then as far as you are concerned, it is not there. The only path we would choose would be among the options shown to us, says Eckles. Thanks to our smartphones, many of our decisions "are going to happen automatically and mindlessly, outside of our awareness".

There is a more serious side to this than merely choosing our eateries. Take the iPhone: Apple decides what will and will not run on it, and vetoes anything it believes is offensive, unsuitable or competitive with its other services. It remains to be seen whether other smartphone manufacturers will follow suit.

A Greater Part of Daily Life

What is clear is that apps are set to become an ever greater part of our lives. As the technology of handsets improves, the next wave of apps will join up the real and virtual worlds even more. Many will be based on "augmented reality", which involves overlaying computer graphics on a view of the real world captured through the phone's camera. In the Android marketplace, apps such as Wikitude and Layar already use the handset's video camera, directional sensors, location information and Internet connection to allow users to look "through" their phones to see a virtually augmented building or landscape. Once developers tap into the full capabilities of the latest version of the iPhone, a flood of similar apps is likely to emerge in Apple's App Store, says Blair MacIntyre of Georgia Institute of Technology in Atlanta, an authority on augmented reality.

That's just the first step, though. Imagine what will be possible when somebody finally manages to commercialise an augmented-reality display built into a pair of high-tech glasses, says Eckles. Though these kinds of displays have been in the works for a while, it is apps that could give the prototypes a final push to the market. Such a display could be connected to "always on" apps, constantly feeding information that overlays our vision, from location-specific tourist information to the nutritional content of our groceries. And when this happens, says Eckles, our smartphones will truly have become the sole lens through which we view the world.

Friday 11:45 p.m.

Lower incisors: sparkling. The toothbrush timer finishes. "You are awesome!" it announces. I smile, but a splinter of suspicion slides into my mind that I may be placing too much store on what my iPhone apps tell me. Maybe my wife is right that I should give it a rest for a while. While pondering the thought, I open up the App Store and check for shaving apps.

•

| "*Having one device try to do it all is an attractive idea, but it often doesn't work out as well in practice as it sounds in theory.*"

Smartphones Are Becoming Too Complex

Debra Littlejohn Shinder

Debra Littlejohn Shinder is a technology consultant, trainer, and author of numerous books on computer operating systems and networking. In the following viewpoint, Shinder maintains that as smartphones gain innovative technologies and functionality, they become more complex, resulting in numerous issues and problems. Options and features added to their operating systems make interfaces more complicated to use, which may frustrate users, she argues. Also, complexity can negatively affect performance, from battery life to mobile services, Shinder continues, as well as compromise the device's security. According to Shinder, one potential solution lies with the tablet, which she says is better suited to perform advanced tasks and can reverse the trend of complex smartphones.

As you read, consider the following questions:

1. Why must each generation of smartphones do more than the previous one, in the author's view?

2. Why do smartphones with complex systems have more security vulnerabilities, as described by Shinder?

3. What other direction can smartphones go to solve the complexity issue, as offered by Shinder?

If you compare today's cell phones (even the less expensive feature phones that are only considered "semi-smart") to the first smartphones, you'll be amazed at how far the technology has come in such a short time.

A Very Brief History of Smartphones

The earliest smartphones were introduced in the early 1990s. This included IBM's Simon and Nokia's Communicator series. The Nokia models were sophisticated, but expensive compared to other brands.

The first touch screen smartphone to run the Symbian operating system was released in 2000 by Ericsson. The Ericsson R380's screen was monochrome, and it had no speaker, headphone jack, expansion card slot, Bluetooth, camera, or GPS [global positioning system]. It did support e-mail and SMS [short message service] and included organizer, voice, memo, and calculator software. You couldn't install your own apps.

Next came the Palm phones, which added voice calling to Palm's popular PDA [personal digital assistant], the PalmPilot. RIM [Research in Motion] came out with the BlackBerry in 2002, and it gained a large customer base, especially among business users. Pocket PC phones evolved from its Windows CE [Embedded Compact]-based PDAs, such as the iPAQ. Windows mobile devices were very much like tiny Windows PCs [personal computers]. But the stylus-centric design made them less user friendly than many people liked.

It was the release of the iPhone in 2007 that really brought smartphones into the mainstream. Android, released the next year, has slowly made inroads to become the overall number one smartphone OS [operating system] in the United States, but the competition is heavy, with new players such as a completely revamped Windows phone operating system (Windows Phone 7) and HP's [Hewlett-Packard's] WebOS, acquired from Palm.

The Complexity Conundrum

With all of this innovation, each generation of smartphones must do more than the one before—users expect new features and capabilities if they're going to spend money to upgrade to the latest version. However, the added functionality means added complexity as well. Some of the negative consequences include user frustration, slowdowns in performance, and security vulnerabilities. Let's take a closer look at each of these consequences and examine how they impact today's smartphones.

Frustrated Users. One of the biggest complaints about the Windows Mobile operating system was that it was too complicated and difficult to use. Even though the interface was very similar to that of the Windows desktop PCs with which most people were familiar, navigating the tiny screen via crowded menus and toolbars just didn't work well. The simplicity of the iPhone's interface has often been credited with its overwhelming success.

Nonetheless, many former iPhone users (along with former Windows Mobile users) have flocked to Android, which offers more options and more ways of doing things. Simplicity necessarily limits functionality to some degree. As Apple scrambles to add new features in order to capture back some of that market, its phones will inevitably slowly become a little more complex, too.

Users really want to have their cake (i.e., a drop-dead simple user interface that's so intuitive a five-year-old can navigate it without instructions) and be able to eat up all the same functions they get with a full-fledged computer, such as the ability to add storage space, view Flash video, and change out their batteries. It's a difficult balance to strike.

Performance Issues. Complexity can also lead to performance issues. For instance, the first iPhones didn't support multitasking for third-party apps. Apple finally added it in iOS 4.0, but many developers have noted that it's not true 100% multitasking; that is, all system resources aren't available to all apps. Some apps can run as background services; some are only paused and then resumed.

Android phones likewise suspend apps that aren't visible to the user, or run a service for background processing. Apple restricts the use of background services that use the network, GPS, and other phone-related resources, in order to conserve battery life. Android doesn't have this restriction—but as a result, apps that use those power-intensive types of resources can run down the battery quickly. The limited memory on smartphones (and the lack of virtual memory in the form of a swap file) leads to performance problems if too many programs are running at once, unless a "kill switch" is implemented to shut down apps that use too much memory. . . .

Security Vulnerabilities. As a system becomes more complex, the potential entry points for breach of security increase. A fortress is easier to protect because it's simpler: It has no windows, few doors, no skylights, or vent systems through which an intruder might sneak. A building with complexities of design and function is more difficult to secure because there are many more potential entryways. Software is the same: Complex code creates more opportunities for hackers and attackers.

What's the Solution?

For the past 15 years or more, we've seen phones become more and more complex, until we can now use them to view and send e-mail, view and compose documents and spreadsheets, take and edit photos, track all sorts of information, read books, scan bar codes, and even pay our bills at points of sale via near field communication.

We've also recently seen the rise of a new form factor that fills the gap between laptop and smartphone: the slate-style tablet. It started with the iPad, which sold like hotcakes to consumers and has even started making some inroads into the business world. Now other vendors are coming out with tablets, many of which are designed with the enterprise in mind, in a variety of sizes and running different operating systems. The tablets range from the 5-inch Dell Streak running Android to the 12-inch Asus Eee Slate running Windows 7.

The larger displays and more roomy virtual keyboards on tablets make them more suitable for some of the tasks for which we've been using our smartphones. With the smaller and lighter tablets, little is sacrificed in terms of portability. Many early adopters of the smaller tablets are carrying them almost everywhere, since they'll fit into a large jacket pocket or a very small bag. In fact, according to many fellow Galaxy Tab enthusiasts I've heard from, the 7-inch size of the Tab— even more than the expandability and openness advantages of the Android OS in comparison to the iOS—was a primary factor in their decision to choose the Tab over the iPad.

If more people carry tablets along with their phones on a daily basis, this could lead to a reversal in the trend of increased complexity in phones. Tablets could take over the more complex tasks, such as composing documents, browsing the web, and viewing or presenting multimedia. Phones could return to more basic functionality, such as talking, texting, and reading e-mail.

Having one device try to do it all is an attractive idea, but it often doesn't work out as well in practice as it sounds in theory—as many owners of all-in-one multi-function printer/copier/scanner/fax machines can attest. The products work, but they generally don't do any of those tasks quite as well as separate, dedicated devices. As more tablet models become available and prices come down, many people are likely to opt for a simpler phone plus a tablet, instead of looking for more and more features in their next phones.

There's also another direction this could go, with smartphones morphing into tablets. Recent "big screen" phone models such as the Droid X and the HTC EVO have proven very popular, and many customers have complained that the Tab and other tablets don't have voice-calling capabilities in the United States.

For those who want a single-device-for-everything solution, there's no technological reason that couldn't be a tablet-sized phone. Sure, a 7-inch device might be awkward to speak into, but many of us already use Bluetooth headsets for most of our calling now, rather than holding the phone up to our faces.

"Is the smartphone—like Google, TV, comics and the movies before it—actually making us dumb?"

Help! My Smartphone Is Making Me Dumb—or Maybe Not

Brian X. Chen

In the following viewpoint, Brian X. Chen asserts that the smartphone and its "always-on network" enable some individuals to multitask effectively. Contrary to research claiming that these technologies have only negative effects on concentration and memory, he says, other studies demonstrate that humans do have the capability to juggle their attention between activities. Indeed, Chen suggests, some experts point out that multitasking is not unique to technologies like smartphones, and research is still inconclusive regarding the effects of digital multitasking on the brain. Chen is a technology reporter for the New York Times *and author of* Always On: How the iPhone Unlocked the Anything-Anytime-Anywhere Future—and Locked Us In.

As you read, consider the following questions:

1. What issue of causality arises with the Stanford University study supporting the negative effects of multitasking, as told by the author?

2. How did "supertaskers" perform in a University of Utah study, as described by the author?

3. What examples of multitasking with very little technology does the viewpoint offer?

Chicago resident Matt Sallee's life is a never-ending sprint that mostly takes place in his phone. At 5 in the morning the alarm goes off, and during his train commute the 29-year-old rolls through 50 e-mails he received overnight on his BlackBerry.

As a manager of global business development at an LED company, Sallee works in time zones spanning three continents.

"I love having 10 different things cooking at once, but for me it's all moving in little pieces, and when it comes time that there are big deliverables needed, I don't have to scramble at the last minute," Sallee said. "It's an hour of combining all the little pieces into one thing, and it's done."

It's not news the "always-on network" is eradicating the borders between home and office, and changing the way people work and play. But how much distraction can one person take? Research is still in the early stages, and there is little hard evidence that 24/7 access to information is bad for you. But the image of frantic, distracted workers scrabbling harder than ever for ever-diminishing social and economic returns is an attractive target for critics.

Not only is it annoying to see people chatting on cell phones in the popcorn line at the cinema, these devices—and the multitasking they encourage—could be taking a massive toll on our psyches, and perhaps even fundamentally altering the way our brains are wired, some dystopian-minded critics suggest.

Is the smartphone—like Google, TV, comics and the movies before it—actually making us dumb?

Fractured Concentration?

Some of the latest arguments to critique this 24/7 online culture include the book *The Shallows* by Nicholas Carr, who argues that the Internet is rewiring us into shallow, inattentive thinkers, along with a *New York Times* feature series by Matt Richtel titled "Your Brain on Computers," a collection of stories examining the possible negative consequences of gadget overload. *(Disclosure: I'm currently writing a book called* Always On *that explores similar topics.)*

Giving credence to such claims, an oft-cited Stanford study published last year found that people who were rated "heavy" multitaskers were less able to concentrate on a single task and also worse at switching between tasks than those who were "light" multitaskers.

"We have evidence that high multitaskers are worse at managing their short-term memory and worse at switching tasks," said Clifford Nass, a Stanford University professor who led the study. He's the author of the upcoming book *The Man Who Lied to His Laptop: What Machines Teach Us About Human Relationships.*

One test asked students to recall the briefly glimpsed orientations of red rectangles surrounded by blue rectangles. The students had to determine whether the red rectangles had shifted in position between different pictures. Those deemed heavy multitaskers struggled to keep track of the red rectangles, because they were having trouble ignoring the blue ones.

To measure task-switching ability, another test presented participants with a letter-and-number combination, like *b6* or *f9*. Subjects were asked to do one of two tasks: One was to hit the left button if they saw an odd number and the right for an even; the other was to press the left for a vowel and the right for a consonant.

They were warned before each letter-number combination appeared what the task was to be, but high multitaskers responded on average half-a-second more slowly when the task was switched. The Stanford study is hardly undisputed. A deep analysis recently published by *Language Log*'s Mark Liberman criticized the study for its small sample group: Only 19 of the students who took the tests were deemed "heavy multitaskers."

He added that there also arises an issue of causality: Were these high multitaskers less able to filter out irrelevant information because their brains were damaged by media multitasking, or are they inclined to engage with a lot of media because they have easily distractible personalities to begin with?

"What's at stake here is a set of major choices about social policy and personal lifestyle," Liberman said. "If it's really true that modern digital multitasking causes significant cognitive disability and even brain damage, as Matt Richtel claims, then many very serious social and individual changes are urgently needed."

"Before starting down this path, we need better evidence that there's a real connection between cognitive disability and media multitasking (as opposed to self-reports of media multitasking)," he added. "We need some evidence that the connection exists in representative samples of the population, not just a couple of dozen Stanford undergraduates enrolled in introductory psychology."

Other research also challenges the conclusions of the Stanford study. A University of Utah study published this year discovered some people who are excellent at multitasking, a class whom researchers dubbed "supertaskers."

Researchers Jason Watson and David Strayer put 200 college undergrads through a driving simulator, where they were required to "drive" behind a virtual car and brake whenever its brake lights shone, while at the same time performing various tasks, such as memorizing and recalling items in the correct order and solving math problems.

Watson and Strayer analyzed the students based on their speed and accuracy in completing the tasks. The researchers discovered that an extremely small minority—just 2.5 percent (three men and two women) of the subjects—showed absolutely no performance loss when performing dual tasks versus single tasks. In other words, these few individuals excelled at multitasking.

Also in contrast with the results of the Stanford study, the supertaskers were better at task-switching and performing individual tasks than the rest of the group.

The rest of the group, on the other hand, did show overall degraded performance when handling dual tasks compared to a single task, suggesting that the vast majority of people might indeed be inadequate at processing multiple activities. But the discovery of supertaskers argues with the ever-popular notion that human brains are absolutely not meant to multitask, Watson and Strayer say, and it shows that this area of research is still very much unexplored.

"Our results suggest that there are supertaskers in our midst—rare but intriguing individuals with extraordinary multitasking ability," Watson and Strayer wrote. "These individual differences are important, because they challenge current theory that postulates immutable bottlenecks in dual-task performance."

Born to Multitask

If the multitasking naysayers claim we're being drowned in data, the same can't be said of their studies. In fact, the research is far too early to be conclusive, argues Vaughan Bell, a neuropsychologist and clinician at the Universidad de Antioquia, Colombia.

"The idea that new technology is 'overloading us' in some way is as old as technology," he said. "Secondly, the idea that 'technology is damaging the brain' in some way just isn't borne out by the evidence."

Bell points out that multitasking is hardly a problem of the digital age—we've been doing it all along. We can dribble a basketball while running, jot down notes while listening to a lecture, and jog through the park while listening to music.

"If you think Twitter is an attention magnet, try living with an infant," Bell said. "Kids are the most distracting thing there is, and when you have three or even four in the house it is both impossible to focus on one thing—and stressful, because the consequences of not keeping an eye on your kids can be frightening even to think about."

(Kids are indeed distracting: A British study found that for drivers, the distraction of squabbling kids can slow down brake-reaction times by 13 percent—as much as alcohol.)

Bell added that residents of poorer neighborhoods that use very little technology (like Medellin, Colombia, where he resides) hardly live distraction-free lives. They have to watch their food because there is no timer; washing clothes has to be done by hand while keeping an eye on everything else; street vendors pass by the house and shout what they're selling, and if you miss that your family could go without food for a day. In short, the 24/7 multitasking lifestyle is nothing new, because for centuries, everywhere in the world there have been a multitude of demands competing for our attention resources, Bell said.

Both Bell and Stanford's Nass do agree on one major misconception: To say that the brain has been "damaged" as a result of multitasking is a dangerously inaccurate statement. The brain, after all, is supposed to change every moment of every day, because that's just what it does. A truly "damaging" effect on the brain can only be demonstrated by gross changes seen in the organ such as obvious tissue lesion or atrophy, Bell said.

A solid consensus on digital multitasking is unlikely to be reached anytime soon, perhaps because the Internet and technology are so broadly encompassing, and there are so many different ways we consume media. Psychological studies have seen a mix of results with different types of technology. For example, some data shows that gamers are better at absorbing and reacting to information than non-gamers. In contrast, years of evidence suggest that television viewing has a negative impact on teenagers' ability to concentrate. The question arises whether tech-savvy multitaskers could consume different types of media more than others and/or be affected in different ways.

A research paper authored by a group of cognitive scientists titled "Children, Wired: For Better and for Worse" sums it up best:

> "One can no more ask, 'How is technology affecting cognitive development?' than one can ask, 'How is food affecting physical development?'" the researchers wrote. "As with food, the effects of technology will depend critically on what type of technology is consumed, how much of it is consumed, and for how long it is consumed."

Hooked on Social Media

Researchers are continuing to examine the effects of multitasking on our ability to focus, but another soon-to-be-published study offers a glimpse into a potentially negative social change in the smartphone era. University of Kansas researchers recently polled a group of 348 students and found that most of them (83 percent) believed that texting while driving was unsafe—even more unsafe than talking on the phone while driving—but 98 percent of them admitted to doing it anyway. The study's 89-item questionnaire asked students to rate perceived risks of different types of texting (initiating a text or replying to one) as well as texting during various driving conditions. Most interesting, the study found that students rated driving on the highway to be intensely risky, but most drivers reported they were just as likely to initiate a text while driving on the highway as they would while driving in normal road conditions. In other words, they were able to convince themselves that road conditions were safer, which made it justifiable to text.

"People know it's harmful, and yet they keep doing it, and they tell themselves they have to do it," said Paul Atchley, an associate professor of psychology who led the study.

Atchley chalks this behavior up to the theory of cognitive dissonance: when you persuade yourself that a behavior is less risky by engaging in it—similar to how the perceived risk of smoking declines in smokers, or the perceived risk of drunk driving decreases when people drive drunk.

But why do people feel they have to text while driving? Social networking sites coupled with a constant Internet connection everywhere you go support the need for individuals to belong, and some research has shown that exclusion from social networks and text messaging can reduce the feeling of belonging. In short, we grow attached to the lifestyle of being always on, and we want to stay plugged in—even when it's a bad idea.

"We're social organisms. There're so many mechanisms built into the brain that are designed for socialization," he said. "The telecommunications industry has hit on something we're built to do."

> *"An iPhone, BlackBerry, or Android-based smartphone will do it all. There's just one problem. Interruptions."*

Smartphones Are a Distraction

Joe Golton

In the following viewpoint, Joe Golton argues that smartphones and their technologies interrupt users' attention, affecting productivity and engagement in activities. Unlike the landline telephone, these devices are carried virtually all the time with constant alerts for texts, e-mails, and social networking notifications, he says, and distracted users compulsively check smartphones for information and updates. To reduce interruptions, he recommends disabling alerts and connectivity, using other devices for reading, and placing smartphones out of reach. Based in San Francisco, California, the author is managing member at Synergy Management Services and creator of FilterJoe, a blog dedicated to reducing distractions in the digital age.

As you read, consider the following questions:

1. How do social norms enable smartphones to cause interruptions, in Golton's view?

2. In what ways do users self-induce interruptions, according to Golton?

3. As stated by the author, what do studies show about interruption technologies?

Over the past few years, excitement has been growing for the idea of an "everything device" that you carry in your pocket. Why carry many separate physical and electronic devices for your phone, address book, calendar, planner, GPS [global positioning system], books, magazines, etc.? An iPhone, BlackBerry, or Android-based smartphone will do it all.

There's just one problem.

Interruptions.

Interruption Technology

Just 15 years ago, interruption technology was mostly confined to the landline telephone. People used this interruption technology sparingly, calling businesses and homes at "reasonable" hours. And many people had rules for keeping interruptions to a minimum, such as my parents' rule of not answering the phone during dinner.

Fast-forward to 2011. Most people carry a cell phone at all times. Voice calls are now just one small part of an ongoing stream of interruptions. Many people set their phones to alert them for each incoming text, instant message, calendar event, and/or e-mail. Some go further with social status notifications from Twitter or Facebook, while others may want to be alerted every time a friend is nearby or their favorite team gets a score.

In addition to all of these "pushed" interruptions, there are self-induced interruptions. It's all too tempting to frequently check (or "pull") weather, scores, stock prices, etc. Many people elect to keep pushed interruptions to a minimum, but then obsessively check their smartphones. Whether self-induced or pushed, an interruption is an interruption.

On top of all this, social norms restraining interruptions have largely disappeared. Though some people with phones allow interruptions sparingly, many others check their phones constantly wherever they are, even while conversing, dining, or driving.

Interruptions are not just an issue with smartphones. Computers are becoming more distracting with alerts, notifications, animations, pop-up ads, and the ever-present temptation to multitask unrelated activities. Numerous studies find that computers, smartphones, or any other form of interruption technology challenges our ability to do anything that requires sustained attention, such as reading, writing, working, playing, and conversing.

Clearly there are many types of interruption technology and they impact many of our activities. But most people carry phones, and many people spend quite a bit of their time reading. So let's take a closer look at trying to read on a smartphone.

Reading on a Smartphone

How do you read on a smartphone, a device that constantly interrupts you?

You don't. Okay, that's a little strong. Phones such as the iPhone or Galaxy S display crystal clear text and have software that makes reading a breeze. They're great for texts, tweets, short e-mails, short posts from your RSS or news reader ... and any other small chunk of text that doesn't require sustained attention to absorb. Some people have no problems reading longer text, even entire novels. But for many people it's hard to read and fully absorb more than a few hundred words on a device that constantly interrupts you or tempts you to interrupt yourself.

What you *can* do is either turn off the interruptions or use a *different* device, the *right* device, for extended reading.

Turning Off Your Phone's Interruptions

You can turn off interruptions on any kind of phone by simply disabling all alerts and connectivity. iPhones or Android devices have airplane mode. BlackBerries have a silent profile. Less sophisticated phones usually have a way to turn off cell phone reception.

Airplane or silent modes are typically used to preserve battery life and/or silence phones in theaters or places of worship. Turn off the interruptions and you may be able to read for as long as you like. How often have you heard people say they catch up on their reading on long airplane flights?

Silencing a phone may work well for some, but others may not want to be cut off completely from the rest of the world while reading. With a bit of fiddling, it is possible to configure some smartphones to only let through certain types of important phone calls or alerts. Reducing interruptions to just a few times per week would make for a reasonable reading experience, I would think.

Use a Different Device for Reading

I've tried turning off my BlackBerry's interruptions. It didn't help. I simply checked more frequently for voice mails, e-mails, etc. Apparently, I've trained myself over the past decade to use my cell phone as an interruption device, no matter how smart or dumb it is. It's not an easy habit to break, even if I wanted to.

My solution: Use a different device for reading.

I acknowledge that my smartphone is an interruption device not suitable for reading at length. I confine my interruptions to this one device. And I set it out of reach when reading something long or doing anything else that requires sustained attention such as writing, conversing, or eating dinner.

Which device is best for reading? In my case, it's an iPod Touch. What's best for you will depend on your preferences for size, display type, battery life, price, and most importantly the kind of reading you do. For some people this may be an iPod Touch or color tablet. For others it may be an E-Ink device like the Nook or Kindle. And for some the traditional printed book is best. I suggest experimenting, taking note of what works best for you for sustained reading.

Interruption Technology in My Own Life

While writing and revising this [viewpoint] over the past month, an interesting thing happened. I became ever more aware of interruptions from my BlackBerry, mostly self-induced. I came to think of it as an interruption device. And I changed.

I now follow the two-device strategy. I repurposed my iPod Touch into a reading device, by moving everything off the home screen that wasn't related to reading or settings. And I no longer use my BlackBerry for anything that requires sustained attention.

Here's the best part: I move my BlackBerry out of reach when I don't want interruptions. At dinner, it's 10 feet away. When working, it's 5 feet away. When reading, I put the Black-Berry in its charging cradle, which flips it into interruption-free bedside mode.

I like the results. I'm getting distracted less and sustaining attention more. Fewer interruptions mean better attention when I read, write, work, play, talk, or eat.

Now that I think of my phone as my one and only "interruption device," I can set aside interruptions any time I want. It's simple. Just move the phone.

> "Smart phones make possible everywhere
> learning, all-the-time learning."

Smartphones Will Benefit Classroom Learning

Elliot Soloway, interviewed by David Nagel

Elliot Soloway is founder and chief executive officer of GoKnow Mobile Learning Solutions, an education consultancy. David Nagel is an executive producer for 1105 Media. In the following viewpoint, Soloway discusses with Nagel how smartphones are integral to the future of education and learning. He describes the devices as a "game changer" because they are the technology of choice for students; they are unrivaled in portability and affordable, as well as capable of performing most tasks and assignments. As demonstrated by the success of pilot programs, Soloway concludes, schools and educators must not resist but adopt smartphones in the classroom.

As you read, consider the following questions:

1. In Soloway's opinion, for students, why do smartphones trump devices with larger screens and keyboards?

2. What examples does Soloway provide of smartphones proving learning in context?

3. Why does Soloway stick to the prediction that every student will have a mobile learning device by 2016?

Within five years, every K–12 student in America will be using a mobile handheld device as a part of learning, according to Elliot Soloway, a professor at the University of Michigan.

"Smart phones are the one technology that can eliminate the digital divide," he told *THE Journal*. "Given the cost of the device, it is very conceivable that every child, rich or poor, can have one 24/7."

Soloway is founder and chief executive officer of GoKnow [Mobile Learning Solutions], an education consultancy that provides professional development seminars for educators, and a member of the faculty in the College of Engineering, the School of Education, and the School of Information at U Mich. He's been following education technology trends for the last three decades, focusing especially on mobile devices for the bulk of those years.

A frequent speaker on education technology issues and a fierce ed tech advocate, Soloway explained that mobile phones are ideal for K–12 students: They're the tool of choice for that generation; they're relatively affordable; they're appropriate 21st-century tools for developing 21st-century skills; and, maybe most significant of all, they enable more than just anytime, anywhere learning. They enable, as Soloway put it, "Everywhere, all-the-time learning."

A Game Changer

David Nagel: You've described the cell phone as a "game changer" for education and as the "quintessential 21st-century tool." Why the cell phone specifically?

Elliot Soloway: There are several reasons why the cell phone is a game changer: It is the device of choice by students—the kids themselves are bringing the devices to school—we adults brought laptops into schools, and they are a yawn, as are netbooks because the kids see cell phones as their generation's technology.

The students are highly competent with the technology; the learning curve is very low. The kids can use the skills they have developed outside of school inside of school.

Portability: The small devices fit into your hand, your pocket, your purse. Portability trumps everything—bigger screen, more power, bigger keyboard. Being able to take it out and turn it [on] instantly is totally important to the mobile, instant gratification generation. The students play all sorts of games on small screens; they are comfortable with small screens. Kids are comfortable with the small keyboards; they have learned to thumb type. Give a kid a full-sized keyboard, and you will reduce the kid to hunt and peck.

Portability provides learning in context—while doing an experiment, [a student] can write it up; while on a field trip, [a student] can capture ideas. And portability enables relating abstract concepts in the classroom to concrete items in the world. For example, what is a complementary angle? What is an isosceles triangle? Well, take a picture after school of objects that illustrate those properties.

The small size matches the small size of the kids: Kids are small; their technology complements their size. Hulking, 7-pound laptops are seen as old technology, not interesting, by the mobile generation: They want to use their technology literally on the go. Can't do that with a laptop.

Laptops are way too expensive to maintain: Drop a laptop, kiss it goodbye; drop a smart phone, and there is a very good chance it will be fine.

You can do everything on a smart phone that you can do on a laptop, except maybe for high school geometry and except for a few scientific visualizations. But for 90 percent of what a student has to do, the smart phone can do it. Why do you need more than that in the palm of your hand, 24/7? And that is using today's screen form factor. Tomorrow we will be able to pull out a screen or we will be able to project a larger screen onto a blank surface. In fact, Samsung's Galaxy already has a version that can shoot out a 60-inch image!

Smart phones make possible everywhere learning, all-the-time learning.

Smart phones are the one technology that can eliminate the digital divide—given the cost of the device, it is very conceivable that every child, rich or poor, can have one 24/7.

What the kids can do and how the kids can do it has changed. For the first time in history, there is a device at a student-affordable price point that has sufficient computing power and networking to support 90 to 95 percent of what a student does in school every day.

Android- and iOS-based slates share a lot of characteristics with cell phones, and they're starting to be adopted more and more in higher ed, especially the iPad at this point. What are the implications for K–12?

What problem does an iPad solve? While they are being adopted, it isn't clear to me or my colleague [GoKnow chief education architect] Cathy Norris why there is such a rush to iPads. They are expensive [and] fragile, and creating content is a challenge. Since learning is all about creating, it seems like a funny device to focus educational attention on. But, it is beautiful, and everyone wants to be part of something beautiful.

Today, in the PC [personal computer] world, whether a computer is a Dell, a Gateway, a Sony, etc., one puts a layer of software on that device, and then from a user's perspective all those different devices are the same. That is what is going to happen shortly in the mobile device space. Different companies are going to build a layer of software that makes every

Important to Teachers, Important to Students

Jarrod Robinson is a physical education and mathematics teacher in Victoria, Australia. Since the beginning of 2008, he has been using his students' mobile phones for mobile activities of polling, audio recording, and most recently QR [quick response] codes in his physical education and mathematics classrooms. . . .

The main reason Robinson chose to start utilizing mobile phones was based on his personal interest in using them in everyday life. "I acknowledged that it had a major role in the organisation of my life, from contacting people through to recording life's moments," he says. "This in itself was enough to have me consider the potential for their use within the classroom. If a mobile phone was important to me, then it sure would be just as important to my students. So why would I deny them the opportunity to use them?"

Liz Kolb, "Case Studies from Math and Science Classrooms: Case Study 13, Jarrod Robinson," Cell Phones in the Classroom: A Practical Guide for Educators. Eugene, OR: International Society for Technology in Education, 2011, p. 87.

smart phone—Android, [Windows Phone 7], iOS, etc.—appear the same to the teacher and the student.

The Only Problem

We have some problems with cell phones as universal tools for students and educators, don't we? What do you think the biggest hurdles are? Policy? Cost of the devices? Reliable and affordable service? Software?

The only problem with mobile devices is perception. "The screen is too small; the keyboard is too small." "I never used one of those devices when I was in school." "The kids are going to cheat." "The phone causes disruptions in the class."

Those are the common negatives we hear.

Those are all easily addressable.

Turn off texting, and turn off voice functions—the smart phone is now truly a computer.

Use the students' tools for learning just like we used students' tools in previous generations for learning—I learned with paper and pencil, since that was the technology of my day. The technology of today is mobile—that's how kids need to learn. We need to prepare kids for the 21st century, not the 19th century.

Cost? Cost is dropping—the calculator was expensive at the outset. But over the next five years, the cost will drop to $5 to $10 per month for the device, the data plan, the software . . . everything. . . . That is definitely affordable. No more paper copying; no more paper textbooks. Cost is not an issue; cost is a phony issue. Even today the cost is not particularly high, compared with putting in a Wi-Fi network capable of supporting 1:1. That is expensive.

What will need to happen to overcome these issues?

We need to accept the fact that mobile technologies are an integral part of the kids' lives and an integral part of 21st-century knowledge workers' lives. We need to stop looking at the past and look to the future. We need to step forward and say: We need to do 21st-century education in the same ways we are doing 21st-century commerce, 21st-century health, etc. There are risks, absolutely. But staying where we are in schools—using 19th-century technology and fooling ourselves that we are teaching 21st-century skills and content—is truly doing our students a huge disservice. You can't teach 21st-century skills and content with 18th-century paper and pencil tools.

A Mobile Learning Device for Every Child

What will be the impact of 4G [referring to the fourth genera-tion of mobile communications standards for cell phones] and mobile broadband for K–12, and what else do you see on the ho-rizon in terms of advancements to the technology of mobile phones?

4G will make it cheaper to use the data plans. The in-creased speed is important, but the reliability is more impor-tant. If we want to do cloud computing, we need always-on connectivity—and that isn't here yet. The need for always-on should be the driver, not faster speeds—that are still unreli-able! Cloud computing and mobile technologies are the yin-yang, two totally intertwined technologies. Once we have reli-able connections then cloud computing will take off. And then a student—or anybody—can do their "work" from any-place because the information—their information—is avail-able everywhere. I really don't like the notion of anywhere, anytime learning. That is too limited. Cathy and I favor the terms "everywhere learning, all-the-time learning." Adults do those two things; that's just what a 21st-century knowledge worker does. So, that's what we need to prepare the mobile generation—the children, the youth, of today—for.

It doesn't take a crystal ball to see that mobile technolo-gies are changing—rapidly, faster than any other technology before—our ways of doing things. Having a mobile device in the palm of your hand, connected to the Internet, 24/7 has never been possible before. It is possible now—finally—at a price point that is just about there—just about affordable by all. Can you imagine 7 billion people all with such a device? Currently there are 4.5 billion cell phones and 7 billion people. Mobile technologies are bigger than the Internet. The Internet is just a roadway; if you don't have a car, the roadway is use-less. Mobile technologies are the cars for the Internet roadway. Mobile technologies are giving voice to people who never had voice before.

Cathy and I make the following prediction: Within five years, every child, in every grade, in every school in America will be using a mobile learning device, 24/7. Take that to the bank! Yes, while today, 99 percent of schools ban cell phones, we stick by this prediction. Why? Because mobile technology is as necessary a part of living in the modern world as are air, water, and food. Communications is the hallmark of what it means to be human; mobile devices support communication in new and exciting ways; mobile devices help make us human, help define us as different than plants and animals. Mobile technologies are essential to our lives—outside of school. How can school resist letting mobile devices through the school door? We shouldn't be asking, "Why should schools adopt mobile technologies?" No! We should be asking, "How can schools be so cynical, so backwards-looking, and prevent our children, the children entrusted to the school's care, to be allowed to benefit from a technology that clearly is highly beneficial?" Schools need to take their heads out of the sand, be brave and step forward, and truly help the children entrusted to them. Mobile technologies can make a huge difference in teaching and learning—the pilot projects are demonstrating that fact over and over and over again. Schools need to be on the right side of the 21st century: 1:1, 24/7 mobile device rollouts should be the norm, not the exception.

| "The smartest phones may be the ones we keep outside the classroom."

Smartphones Do Not Benefit Classroom Learning

Maclean's

In the following viewpoint, the editors of Maclean's *oppose the use of smartphones for learning in the classroom. While acknowledging the advantages of electronically delivering textbooks and other materials to students' smartphones and linking classmates together with technology, they argue that handhelds are tools of "mass distraction," encouraging texting, surfing, and other activities that are unrelated to education. In fact, the editors maintain that technologies do not improve academic performance, concluding that smartphones and other devices cannot replace the ability of teachers to engage easily distracted students.* Maclean's *is a Canadian weekly newsmagazine.*

As you read, consider the following questions:

1. What issues must be addressed if cell phones are made part of the official school day, according to the viewpoint?

2. According to the viewpoint, how does the presence of laptops at universities anticipate the presence of cell phones in public schools?

3. What did a study show about the effect of texting on performing simple tasks, as told by *Maclean's*?

The role of technology in the classroom has no doubt been a contentious issue since the first Roman student brought an abacus to his grammaticus. Using the most up-to-date equipment in school has always seemed to be a necessity. And yet the process of learning hasn't really changed that much since ancient times: Teachers still need to teach and students still need to pay attention.

Last week [in September 2010] Ontario premier Dalton McGuinty sparked a national debate on the role of technology in Canadian classrooms. Asked about a proposal to relax a ban on cell phones in the classrooms of Toronto-area high schools, the premier seemed rather agreeable to the idea. "Telephones, BlackBerries and the like are conduits for information and one of the things we want our students to be is well informed," he said. "It's something we should be looking at in our schools."

McGuinty has a point. It seems inevitable that some sort of handheld wireless device will eventually become part of education systems across the country. The cost and complication of traditional textbooks makes electronic delivery of course material straight into the hands of students a rather attractive proposition. For this reason alone, electronic tablets or smartphones such as the BlackBerry likely have a place in the classroom of the future. The prospect of linking students together via communication technology also holds great educational promise.

Too Soon to Advocate Cell Phones in the Classroom

At the same time, we can't ignore the enormous and obvious downsides of such technological intrusions. Cell phones may be conduits for information, but they're also tools of mass distraction. Texting, tweeting, surfing and updating your on-line profile have nothing to do with learning and no place in the classroom. Yet it's even become commonplace for parents to text their children during school hours. What are they thinking?

Any effort to make cell phones part of the official school day must solve the problem of their noneducational use, either by setting strict rules of acceptable conduct or blocking access when it's not appropriate. And we should recognize that there's a big difference between integrating wireless devices into the curriculum and simply inviting students to bring whatever diverting gadgets they might possess to class. The fact that not every student owns a smartphone must also be addressed. Regardless of what the future holds, it's far too soon to be advocating widespread use of cell phones in the classroom.

It's also the case that the value of technology to learning is frequently oversold by eager advocates. A long series of educational revolutions via technology has been promised throughout the years: from television to video to desktop computers to laptops to SMART Boards to cell phones. Despite claims that these innovations will change the educational experience for the better, there's no evidence technology actually leads to higher marks for students.

Technology Will Never Replace Skilled Teachers

The ubiquitous presence of wireless laptops on university campuses in many ways anticipates the presence of cell phones in public schools. A study from 2008 in the academic journal *Computers & Education* looked at how these laptops have affected classroom behaviour. "Results showed that students who used laptops in class spent considerable time multitasking and that laptop use posed a significant distraction to both users and fellow students," the research observes. "Most im-

The Challenge to Exploit the Potential of Smartphones

Almost any technology can be used for good or ill. A pen can write a sonnet or scratch foul language into a desk. Smartphones with their many applications, video and still cameras, note-taking and recording capabilities as well as Internet access are not so much phones as complex devices in which only one function is the phone. Here we have a device of extraordinary potential. In the palm of the hand, it can provide access to information far greater than the largest, traditional paper-based library. Yet it can be a source of distraction, disruption and the means by which youth are hurt. It can be used to digitally capture events for learning, but it can also capture private events. When combined with web spaces like YouTube, it can become anything from a place of public ridicule and degradation to a site of the highest creative expression.... There is a challenge to us to exploit its potential for learning while at the same time ameliorating its potential as a source of distraction, harm, illegal and unethical behaviour.

Sandy Schuck, Peter Aubusson, John Buchanan, and Tom Russell, "The Interactive Whiteboard: Ivan's Vignette," Beginning Teaching: Stories from the Classroom. *New York: Springer, 2012, p. 107.*

portantly, the level of laptop use was negatively related to several measures of student learning." Students with laptops had lower test results than those without. The reason? They were often not paying attention to their teachers. We should expect the same thing from cell phones.

Similarly, a 2009 study looked at students who sent instant messages during class. Texting students took longer to perform simple tasks such as reading a written passage than those who did not. Consider it another blow to the alleged benefits of multitasking. An investigation into PowerPoint lectures found students enjoyed them more than traditional presentations, although this did nothing to raise test scores. Clickers, small handheld wireless devices used for in-class quizzes that are popular with students and teachers, similarly have no discernible impact on marks.

Technology may lower school costs, make marking more efficient and even raise student satisfaction. But it can't produce students with better grades. And this means technology will never replace the timeless need for skilled teachers capable of catching the attention of easily distracted students and engaging their minds. The smartest phones may be the ones we keep outside the classroom.

Periodical and Internet Sources Bibliography

The following articles have been selected to supplement the diverse views presented in this chapter.

Warren Adler	"The Smart Phone Addiction," *Huffington Post*, December 2, 2011.
Tom Chatfield	"Smartphones Lock Us in to Our Own Lives— Art Can Release Us Again," *Independent*, July 13, 2012.
Damon Darlin	"How I Learned to Stop Worrying by Loving the Smartphone," *New York Times*, June 8, 2011.
Mark Frydenberg, Wendy Ceccucci, and Patricia Sendall	"Smartphones: Teaching Tool or Brain Candy?," *Campus Technology*, January 31, 2012.
Anya Kamenetz	"A Is for App: How Smartphones, Handheld Computers Sparked an Educational Revolution," *Fast Company*, April 1, 2010.
Gregory Karp	"A Frugal Ring?," *Chicago Times*, August 19, 2011.
Katy Moeller	"Smartphones: High-Tech Distractions or Good Tools for Idaho Schools?," *Idaho Statesman*, February 11, 2012.
Brad Moon	"Cellphones in the Classroom: Bad Idea, Inevitable, or Both?," *Wired*, September 20, 2010.
John D. Sutter	"Smartphones: Our National Obsession," CNN.com, October 18, 2010.
Damian Thompson	"The New Global Addiction: Smartphones," *Telegraph*, June 15, 2012.

OPPOSING
VIEWPOINTS®
SERIES

Who Owns and Uses Smartphones?

Chapter Preface

According to a 2012 report from the Pew Internet & American Life Project, 23 percent of twelve- to seventeen-year-olds say they have smartphones. Ownership is highest at 31 percent for fourteen- to seventeen-year-olds, compared with 8 percent for twelve- to thirteen-year-olds. "Teens are fervent communicators," states senior research specialist Amanda Lenhart in the report. "Straddling childhood and adulthood, they communicate frequently with a variety of important people in their lives: friends and peers, parents, teachers, coaches, bosses, and a myriad of other adults and institutions."

For some parents, buying their child a smartphone has become a matter of when, not if. Suzanne Kantra, founder and editor in chief of technology website Techlicious, says that she will buy her daughter a smartphone when she turns twelve. Kantra has few qualms about her using it responsibly and safely for schoolwork, getting organized, and enjoying her favorite digital media. "For some kids, this won't be a problem, but others might benefit from the boundaries you can set with parental controls," she says in an article on the *Today* show website. "For things like managing talk time, text messaging, and call blocking, the carriers all have parental controls. For everything else, you'll have to rely on settings you choose on the phone," Kantra continues.

Others, nonetheless, maintain that a twelve-year-old might still be too young for a smartphone. Marguerite Reardon, a senior writer for CNET, suggests that smartphones are more appropriate for teenagers in high school and advises parents to designate an old or cheap feature phone for children to use. "I just think that kids today will have a lifetime of gadgets and cell phones. It won't hurt them to wait another few years before getting one of their own," she claims in a 2011 CNET article. In the following chapter, the authors investigate how ownership of—and reliance on—smartphones is changing.

> "*Smartphone owners are now more prevalent within the overall population than owners of more basic mobile phones.*"

Smartphone Ownership Is Growing

Aaron Smith

In the following viewpoint, Aaron Smith states that smartphone ownership in the United States is rising, with 46 percent of American adults owning the handhelds as of February 2012. The author also observes that almost every demographic saw growth in smartphone penetration; adoption levels reached 60 percent and higher for several groups. Additionally, the percentage of mobile phone users unsure if they own a smartphone has decreased notably, he says. Smith is a senior research specialist for the Pew Internet & American Life Project, focusing on technology in civic life and online interaction with government.

As you read, consider the following questions:

1. What definition of a smartphone owner is offered in the viewpoint?

2. Which chief group has seen modest or no growth in smartphone ownership, as told by Smith?

3. According to Smith, how does age influence smartphone ownership?

Nearly half (46%) of American adults are smartphone owners as of February 2012, an increase of 11 percentage points over the 35% of Americans who owned a smartphone last May. As in 2011, our definition of a smartphone owner includes anyone who said yes to either of the following two questions:

- 45% of cell owners *say that their phone is a smartphone,* up from 33% in May 2011

- 49% of cell owners *say that their phone operates on a smartphone platform* common to the US market, up from 39% in May 2011

Taken together, just over half of cell owners (53%) said yes to one or both of these questions and are classified as smartphone owners. Since 88% of US adults are now cell phone owners, that means that a total of 46% of *all* American adults are smartphone users. Two in five adults (41%) own a cell phone that is not a smartphone, meaning that smartphone owners are now more prevalent within the overall population than owners of more basic mobile phones.

As smartphone ownership has grown over the last year, there has been a corresponding shift in the specific types of phones that Americans report owning:

- 20% of cell owners now describe their phone as an Android device, up from 15% in May 2011

- 19% of cell owners now describe their phone as an iPhone, up from 10% in May 2011

- 6% of cell owners now describe their phone as a Black-Berry, down from 10% in May 2011

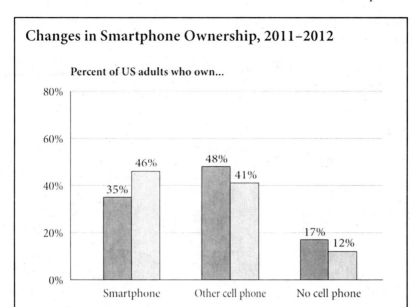

Changes in Smartphone Ownership, 2011–2012

Percent of US adults who own...

- ▓ May 2011
- ☐ February 2012

Source: Pew Research Center's Internet & American Life Project April 26–May 22, 2011 and January 20–February 19, 2012 tracking surveys. For 2011 data, n=2,277 adults ages 18 and older, including 755 interviews conducted on respondent's cell phone. For 2012 data, n=2,253 adults and survey includes 901 cell phone interviews. Both 2011 and 2012 data include Spanish-language interviews.

TAKEN FROM: Aaron Smith, "46% of American Adults Are Smartphone Owners," Pew Internet & American Life Project, March 1, 2012.

The proportion of cell owners describing their phone as a Windows (2%) or Palm (1%) device is unchanged since the last time we asked this question in May 2011.

Smartphone Ownership Has Increased Across a Wide Range of Demographic Groups

Nearly every major demographic group—men and women, younger and middle-aged adults, urban and rural residents, the wealthy and the less well off—experienced a notable uptick in smartphone penetration over the last year, and overall adoption levels are at 60% or more within several cohorts, such as college graduates, 18–35-year-olds and those with an annual household income of $75,000 or more.

Although this overall increase in smartphone ownership is relatively widespread, several groups saw modest or nonexistent growth in the last year. Chief among these are seniors, as just 13% of those aged 65 and older now own a smartphone. This is far below the national average of 46%, and is largely unchanged from the 11% of seniors who were classified as smartphone owners in 2011. Similarly, smartphone adoption among those without a high school diploma grew by a relatively modest seven percentage points over the last year, and overall adoption rates for this group continue to be roughly half of the national average (25% of those without a high school diploma currently are smartphone owners).

African Americans and Latinos also exhibited modest changes in smartphone adoption between our 2011 and 2012 surveys. However, in contrast to those groups, both African Americans and Latinos have overall adoption rates that are comparable to the national average for all Americans (smartphone penetration is 49% in each case, just higher than the national average of 46%).

As we found in our previous study of smartphone adoption, young adults tend to have higher-than-average levels of smartphone ownership regardless of income or educational attainment, while for older adults smartphone ownership tends to be relatively uncommon across the board—but especially so for less educated and affluent seniors. Among 18–29-year-olds there is a 14-point difference in smartphone ownership rates between those earning less than $30,000 per year and those earning more than $30,000 per year (and smartphone ownership even among lower-income young adults is well above the national average). By contrast, for those 65 and older, there is a 22-point difference between these income cohorts (and just 5% of low-income seniors are smartphone users).

Similarly, smartphone ownership decreases dramatically with age even among adults with similar levels of education. However, younger adults with a high school diploma or less are significantly more likely to own a smartphone than even those seniors who have attended college.

Confusion over the Term "Smartphone" Has Declined in the Last Year

As smartphone ownership has become more widespread over the last year, consumers have generally found it easier to answer questions about their phones and whether they own a smartphone or not. To be sure, there is still some confusion around this term as 8% of cell owners are still not sure if their phone is a smartphone. However, this is a significant decrease from the 14% of cell owners who were not sure if their phone was a smartphone or not in May 2011. Similarly, the proportion of cell owners who volunteered that don't know what type of phone they have fell from 13% of cell owners in May 2011 to just 4% of cell owners in February 2012.

> *"Diehards [of outdated cellphone models] say they are reducing waste and . . . sidestepping costly service contracts."*

Some People Reject Smartphone Ownership

Sue Shellenbarger

Sue Shellenbarger writes the Work & Family column for the Wall Street Journal. In the following viewpoint, she explains why some people choose not to own smartphones and cling to outdated models. Preferences for simplicity and lower priced service plans are some main reasons, says Shellenbarger, while other individuals become attached to older cell phone models. Furthermore, she explains that some owners of basic handhelds want to resist the temptation to text and avoid the distractions of smartphones that many believe make users oblivious to their surroundings and the people around them.

As you read, consider the following questions:

1. As cited by the author, how often do consumers rush out to get the latest cell phone?

2. As told by Shellenbarger, why does Daniel Clarkson like not downloading directions on his cell phone?

3. What does Erica Koltenuk state in the viewpoint about communication and mobile phones?

Julie Barbour-Issa calls her eight-year-old cellphone "the dinosaur. It's a brick, and I could use it as a weapon in an emergency," says the 30-year-old Norwood, Mass., civil engineer.

The screen on her Nokia 6010 got a star-shaped crack when it was dropped on a rock after an office Christmas party four years ago. It's embarrassing to whip it out at family gatherings, she says, where relatives have all the latest smartphones. Even buried deep in her purse, the phone has an antiquated "beepity-beep" ringtone that embarrasses her. "My friends say, 'I had that phone back when it was cool—10 years ago,'" says Ms. Barbour-Issa, who is currently an at-home mom. She missed a hike with her friends recently because they set it up spontaneously using their smartphones to message each other on Facebook.

But all that is OK with her, she says. "I hate waste. I don't care if I'm hip. And I'm cheap."

Most consumers rush to get the hot new cellphone—every 17 months on average, according to J.D. Power and Associates, a marketing-information company. Device makers like Apple, Motorola and Nokia—as well as cellphone carriers—constantly advertise the latest models and fastest service. Still, the holdouts cling to obsolete models with clunky designs.

These diehards say they are reducing waste and . . . sidestepping costly service contracts. Some like the simplicity of phones with few functions, says Anthony Scarsella, chief gadget officer at Gazelle, a Boston-based reseller of electronic gear. Others "want to make a statement: 'I don't want the latest and greatest, I want to hold on to what I have,'" Mr.

Featuring No Contracts

It's easy to get a pretty good, no-contract feature phone for $50 or less (or even for free), and then get a month-to-month or prepaid plan that allows web browsing, e-mail, and other data access. That costs around $50 per month.

Generally users can cancel these phones at any time, with no early termination fee.

Amy Gahran, "Why Smartphones Still Haven't Taken Over the U.S. Market," CNN.com, August 31, 2011.

Scarsella says. About 6% of the 600,000 gadgets traded on Gazelle's website in the past two years are cellphones over three years old.

David Blumenthal still uses a five-year-old green Samsung flip phone, even after his Welsh terrier chewed the case to "the consistency of an old piece of gum," he says. He tried to buy a replacement cover but couldn't find one. So he put Scotch tape over the back to hold in the battery. "It's a very basic, functioning telephone, and that's what I use it as—a telephone," says the Chestnut Hill, Mass., attorney. Raised in a frugal Maine family, Mr. Blumenthal sees no need to "keep running out and buying new things if you can patch them and they hold together."

Attachments to Certain Models

Others develop an attachment to a certain model, says Joe McKeown, a vice president at ReCellular, an Ann Arbor, Mich., cellphone recycler. Some customers have bought five or six identical models of the original Motorola Razr, an ultra-slim flip phone that was extremely popular six or seven years ago, he says.

Kat Lopez has loved the Samsung Juke ever since she first spotted a turquoise-and-silver model in a Verizon store in 2007. "You flip it open like a switchblade," says the Manhattan, Kan., graduate student. It fits easily in her pocket, but it also flies out easily. She is now on her fifth Juke—one was lost when she was riding a roller coaster. When Samsung stopped making them, she sourced the last two from a college friend and on Amazon for $50.

When friends made fun of her Juke's tiny alphanumeric keypad, asking, "How do you text on that thing? It's so small," Ms. Lopez says, she challenged them to a text-off over dinner and won—by typing and sending an excerpt from the restaurant menu faster than her two friends using smartphones. "I'm so used to it that I don't have to look while I text," she says.

Daniel Clarkson's friends laugh at his eight-year-old Samsung flip phone, which actually has an extendible antenna. But the 31-year-old Memphis federal court clerk likes avoiding the temptation to text or make calls while walking down the street, or download directions while driving. People focused on their smartphones are "so oblivious to their surroundings, they could walk into a car in the street and not realize it," he says. And when Mr. Clarkson drives to an unfamiliar place, "I like the idea that I can look at a map, and get around on my own."

"Don't Want to Be Looking at Our Phones"

For Erica Koltenuk, "the pressure to always be in communication with people is overwhelming," she says. She liked the fact that the battery in the old Motorola Razr flip phone she used for the past 1 1/2 years couldn't hold a charge for more than five minutes. It gave her a good excuse for keeping phone calls short. "I could say, 'Gotta go, my phone is dying,'" says the 25-year-old Salt Lake City teacher, student and wilderness guide. "I think being on the phone or texting prevents you from doing things in the moment."

She has found a kindred spirit in her boyfriend, Patrick Crowley. The last time Mr. Crowley bought a new phone five years ago, he told the salesman, "I want a phone that you could drop-kick into a lake and go get it and still be able to make a call." Mr. Crowley, 32, a hydrologist and cofounder of Chapul Inc., a health food start-up, got a Casio G'zOne, then replaced it with an old, used model off Craigslist two years ago. He uses it only to make calls—and occasionally as a flashlight. When he comes home, he and Erica "don't want to be looking at our phones," he says. "We want to be cooking together and having face-to-face conversations."

"Growing numbers of low-income Americans are relying upon smartphones as their primary means of reaching the Internet."

The Disadvantaged and Minorities Use Smartphones for Internet Access

Gerry Smith

Based in New York, Gerry Smith reports on cybersecurity for the Huffington Post. In the following viewpoint, he claims that more minorities and low-income individuals use smartphones to go online. Recent data shows that African Americans and Latinos are more likely to have smartphones than whites, Smith states, because such handhelds are more affordable than computers and broadband service. Nonetheless, disagreement arises on whether the devices help bridge the digital divide, he points out. The wireless industry believes that smartphones place the Internet and digital economy within greater reach of disadvantaged groups, Smith explains, while critics argue that smartphones are not a viable replacement for computers and more reliable broadband connections.

As you read, consider the following questions:

1. As told by the author, how did Erick Huerta use his iPhone in college before he could afford a laptop?

2. What are the "built-in limits" of smartphones, as described by Smith?

3. What does Jot Carpenter state about the choice between wireless and high-speed Internet service?

When Erick Huerta was growing up in Los Angeles, his family could not afford a computer. His mother sold tamales from a street-side stall, and his father drove a taxi. Huerta and his three sisters were more worried whether their parents could pay rent than whether they could get online.

Yet when Huerta, 27, enrolled at East Los Angeles College, he knew he would need reliable Internet access for his course work. So four years ago [in 2008], he spent $250 of his scholarship money on a piece of technology he could afford: a smartphone. He split the cost of a wireless plan with a friend and used his iPhone for almost everything, from checking e-mail and taking notes to conducting research and writing papers.

The experience typically proved exasperating. Typing papers entailed pecking away for hours on the small screen, an exercise that left his fingers aching and numb. Registering for classes, seeking scholarships and applying for jobs often required visiting websites that were effectively off-limits, unreadable on mobile devices.

The experience was like window shopping, without being able to enter the store and buy the merchandise. "You can see the information that you want, but you can't grasp it fully until you're on a desktop," Huerta says, adding that he recently saved up enough money to buy a laptop computer—a considerable upgrade. "A smartphone does a lot of everything, but it doesn't do enough."

Bridging the Digital Divide?

Huerta's attempt to substitute a smartphone for a full-sized computer represents a trend that some say holds the potential to bridge the digital divide. Growing numbers of low-income Americans are relying upon smartphones as their primary means of reaching the Internet, according to surveys by the Pew Research Center. Yet Huerta's frustration also highlights why this development may fall short of closing the divide, instead of bringing people into contact with a digital medium they cannot fully exploit.

The mobile telecommunications industry portrays smartphones as a progressive force, one that is delivering web access to historically disadvantaged communities. It cites data showing that African Americans and Latinos are now more likely to own smartphones than whites. But as Huerta and others have discovered, mobile devices come with the built-in limits of stripped-down web browsers, offering connections that are typically slower and less reliable than wired broadband links.

"There just isn't adequate bandwidth to hold a video conference call or get an education or get access to telemedicine," says Susan Crawford, a professor at Harvard's Kennedy School of Government. "None of that is realistically possible over a wireless connection on a smartphone."

Smartphones are also prone to running up additional costs, as wireless companies have begun capping how much data customers are allowed to use before extra fees apply.

"If your only access to the Internet is through a phone, you run a much greater risk of having an extra cell phone bill every month," says Amalia Deloney, an associate director at the Center for Media Justice, a nonprofit that works on media policy in low-income and minority communities.

You also run the risk of getting shut out: The web as encountered on a smartphone is a subset of the web as available via a standard computer, depriving those dependent on these smaller devices of often crucial resources.

Many social service agencies that provide aid to poor people—from food stamps to emergency rent assistance—have not formatted their websites for mobile access, presenting a considerable barrier to help, Deloney says.

Only about one-fourth of American companies with websites have enabled them to be easily accessed by mobile devices, according to a survey of 117 U.S. companies by Potentialpark Communications, a market-research firm based in Stockholm.

A smartphone is "an entry point into the digital economy," says Deloney. "It shouldn't in any way, shape, or form be seen as a replacement for a computer and broadband access."

Those Left Behind

For the wireless industry, smartphones have become a primary talking point in making a case that its services amount to a force for social good.

"Because of their relatively low cost and accessibility in low-income communities, handheld devices can help advance digital equity," the Cellular Telecommunications and Internet Association, the wireless industry trade group, declares on its website.

Jot Carpenter, vice president of government affairs for the trade association, dismisses as "incredibly elitist" suggestions that smartphones are less than acceptable stand-ins for computers. He maintains that the devices have become "on-ramps to participating in the Internet economy" for communities traditionally underserved.

"The choice isn't between wireless service and the absolutely highest speed Internet available," Carpenter says. "For many of these people, the choice is between wireless service and no Internet access at all."

For years, policy experts and community activists have debated how best to deliver the promise of technology to those who can least afford it. Despite numerous initiatives aimed at giving every American equal access to computers and Internet, low-income Americans and minorities have fallen behind.

About three-fourths of white households have broadband Internet at home, compared with slightly more than half of all black and Latino households, according to Commerce Department data. Less than half of all American households with incomes below $25,000 have broadband connections at home, compared with 93 percent of homes earning $100,000 or more.

But in surveys of smartphone adoption, such gaps appear to narrow. According to the Pew Internet & American Life Project, 49 percent of blacks and Latinos now own smartphones, compared with 45 percent of whites. About 40 percent of people in households earning less than $30,000 say they go online mostly through their phones, compared with just 17 percent of those earning more than $50,000, according to Pew.

The key driver behind this trend is finance, say experts. Lower-income households have been seizing smartphones as an affordable means of gaining access to the web.

A Primary Target Market

While laptops or PCs [personal computers] may be unaffordable for some people, smartphones tend to be free or heavily discounted when customers sign wireless contracts. Several wireless providers, including MetroPCS and Cricket Wireless, offer prepaid, no-contract plans with unlimited talk, text and web browsing for as little as $40 a month.

S. Craig Watkins, a professor at the University of Texas at Austin who studies the digital habits of teens, has been struck by the clustering of cell phone shops in African American neighborhoods, such as in New York City's Harlem, where he recently surveyed the offerings.

"Almost every fourth or fifth store, you could buy a mobile device or mobile phone," said Watkins, who is black. "But nowhere did I see where you can buy a computer." This, he added, underscores a reality of the market: "Mobile carriers have identified the African American community as a primary target audience for their product."

From 2007 to 2009, Americans collectively saw web access on handheld devices grow by 73 percent, according to the Pew Internet & American Life Project. During those same years, usage by African Americans grew at nearly double that pace—141 percent.

But even as smartphones are clearly bringing the web to minority communities, Watkins is concerned with how people are using that access. Black and Latino youth are more active than whites in using mobile devices to play games, watch videos, listen to music, according to a 2010 Kaiser Family Foundation study.

"Mobile alone does not help people develop those computer and literacy skills that are critical to success in the 21st century," Watkins says.

A Crucial Link

But at Crenshaw High School, a predominantly African American public school in Los Angeles, smartphone web access has become a major conduit for serious academic pursuits. Isaiah Marshall, a junior, has come to rely upon his smartphone as often the only way he can complete his homework assignments. He doesn't have a computer or Internet at home. The school has some computers, but they are nearly always occupied, and some are out of order, he says. So he often sits down at a desk in the library and uses his phone to do research.

"If I didn't have my phone, I would be in a deep hole right now," Marshall says. "I'd be scrambling around trying to find ways to look up research to do this paper, or access this PowerPoint. There would be gaps and holes that I would keep falling in."

Ashley Street, 23, a single mother in Philadelphia, has seen both the promises and pitfalls of relying on smartphones. When Street was briefly homeless and sleeping in a park, she used her phone to find a shelter, she says. When she was laid off from her job at McDonald's, she was able to apply for a new job via her phone's web access.

But when Street recently tried to use her phone to fill out a student aid form so she can attend culinary school, it seemed almost futile. Just as she was nearing the end of the application, the phone's wireless connection failed, and her information disappeared from the screen.

"I had to do it all over again," she says. "I actually almost cried."

On a recent afternoon, Street sat among a dozen other young women in a computer lab at the People's Emergency Center, a social service agency in West Philadelphia. Many of the women have lived in shelters. Only a few own computers. All had smartphones.

The agency gives free netbooks to clients who complete an eight-week computer training course. Yet most have no way of connecting those netbooks to the Internet, says Hamidou Traore, who teaches digital literacy at the center. Traore teaches them how to tether their smartphones—using free apps that turn their phones into Wi-Fi hot spots so they can get Internet access on their netbooks.

"This way they can edit their resumes and send it to employers," Traore says. "They wouldn't be able to do that on their smartphones."

Mobile devices are now being introduced in classrooms across the country. At St. Marys City School District in St. Marys, Ohio—where about half the students qualify for free and reduced lunches—about 500 students in third, fourth and fifth grades use smartphones in the classroom. The devices are installed with educational programs so students can write essays or study math, says Kyle Menchhofer, a technology coordinator for the school district.

The phones serve as a way to give every student equal time on a computer at school. Most district classrooms hold 24 students, he says, but only have four computers.

"If we did not have these devices in the classroom, our low-income students might be getting 15 minutes a week on the computer," Menchhofer says.

Earning a Degree on a Smartphone?

But some teachers have concerns about students relying upon smartphones for their course work.

Brian Steinberg, an instructor at several online colleges, including the University of Phoenix, says about 10 percent of his students attempt to complete their assignments using smartphones—an easy-to-identify group: Their papers are sprinkled with language often reserved for text messages, such as "gr8" and "l8ter," with sentences punctuated with smiley faces.

Steinberg says he believes students are more focused sitting at a desk in front of a computer than when they are staring into a smartphone. Those who use phones for academic papers typically receive lower grades because of typos and grammatical errors.

"You can't get a degree online from your cell phone," Steinberg says. "I don't think it's doable yet."

For months, Oscar Reyes, 20, used his smartphone for his schoolwork at TCI College of Technology, a for-profit college in New York City. Reyes says he couldn't afford a laptop on his $10.75 an hour salary as a butcher.

When he needed to write papers, Reyes used his smartphone to conduct web research, and then dictated essays, using technology on the device that converted speech into text.

But Reyes often struggled with dead spots in his Queens neighborhood, frequently losing access to the web. He used the Internet on his phone for such lengths that he exceeded his wireless provider's data cap, slowing his Internet service to a crawl.

"Once I hit that data cap everything started loading too slowly," Reyes says. "It would take a minute or two to load a page. God forbid if I had to watch a video because then it was impossible."

Reyes found himself envious of friends who had laptops, with their larger screens and the ability to open several web pages at once, while he made do with one at a time.

Recently, he used money from his tax return to purchase a used laptop. It was like opening a portal to a richer world.

"With a laptop you can see everything nice and big and everything is legible and readable," Reyes says. "When I'd look at my phone I'd think, 'I can do about half of that and that's about it.'"

> "As people of color have closed that di-
> vide with their mobile devices, they've
> moved into another uncertain realm."

Smartphones Do Not Improve Internet Access for the Disadvantaged and Minorities

Jamilah King

*In the following viewpoint, Jamilah King argues that telecommu-
nications companies have unregulated power over mobile wireless services, impacting African Americans, Latinos, and the disadvantaged—groups adopting smartphones as the most
affordable way to access the Internet. King asserts that the web is
central to participation in the workforce and civic life, and telecom giants have control over the content and actions of smartphone users. Moreover, broadband access and coverage remain
disproportionate among minorities, she maintains, and corporations seek greater control of the Internet and telecommunications
through consolidation, regulation, and influencing advocacy
groups. King is the news editor at Colorlines.com, a daily news
site focused on race matters.*

As you read, consider the following questions:

1. What figures does King cite for African Americans, Latinos, and whites using only their cell phones to get online?

2. How does the author characterize wireless mobile as the "second Internet"?

3. How did Verizon control the content of customers' cell phones in 2007, as alleged by King?

As the 2011 holiday shopping season geared up, the country's leading mobile wireless carrier, Verizon, announced a special deal. For a limited time only, customers could get the popular HTC Droid Incredible 2 smartphone for free, if they signed up for a two-year data plan. Since the phone's full retail price is usually more than $430, the deal meant a savings of more than $200 with a new contract. It features a four-inch touch screen and eight megapixel rear camera, along with top-of-the-line video and one of the industry's fastest processors. It's everything you need to feel like you've got the Internet in your pocket, and for a fraction of the price of a computer. That's a compelling selling point for many buyers, but particularly so among the black and Latino consumers who are so key to the now massive smartphone market.

There are 234 million cell phone subscribers in the United States, 45.5 million of whom own smartphones. By the end of 2011, the consumer electronics industry is expected to bring in more than $190 billion. The industry's trade group, Consumer Electronics Association, noted in June that smartphone sales are the market's primary driver. They're expected to bring in more than $23 billion in industry revenue this year.

A remarkable share of that revenue is coming from people of color, who are adopting smartphones at faster rates than white consumers and are doing far more with them. Research shows people of color are more likely to surf the Internet, send and receive messages, engage social media and produce or publish media on their phones. The reason for that, many say, is simple: It's the most affordable way to get onto the information superhighway. A couple hundred dollars for an Android and a data plan is much less than $1,000 for a laptop computer and broadband connection.

Verizon, in particular, has targeted the massive and growing market among smartphone users of color, and not just with bargains. In 2010 the company unveiled its "Rule the Air" campaign. One commercial featured a racially diverse cast of women making a series of bold statements, including: "Air has no prejudice. It does not carry the opinions of a man faster than those of a woman." And, "Air is unaware if I'm black or white and wouldn't care if it knew."

The companies selling that air are certainly aware of race, however, particularly those selling Android phones. More than a quarter of black cell phone users have Androids, which is more than twice the number of those who use BlackBerries and five times more than those who use iPhones. (Indeed, Colorlines.com's own audience metrics show that if you're reading this on a mobile device, you're probably holding an Android right now.) In contrast, only 12 percent of white smartphone users prefer Androids. The retail price of the Droid Incredible is over $200 cheaper than the iPhone.

The Bridge Across the Digital Divide

In an increasingly digital world, the relative affordability of smartphones have made them the bridge across the Internet's long-discussed digital divide. Nearly a fifth—18 percent—of African American wireless subscribers use *only* their cell phones to get online, as do 16 percent of Latinos. Just 10 percent of whites say the same. While 33 percent of white subscribers use their cell phones to surf the Internet, 51 percent of Latinos and 46 percent of African Americans do.

"When you look at the groups that are more likely to say that they go online mostly using their cell phone, they tend to be most highly oriented around groups that have not had high levels of broadband adoption," explains Aaron Smith, an analyst at the Pew Research Center's Internet & American Life Project who has studied the smartphone market.

All of this market data is more than information age trivia, though. "Broadband adoption"—or, creating widespread access to high-speed Internet in homes—is arguably the most significant challenge in our political, economic and cultural transition to being a linked-in nation. But the leading solutions for achieving it, both among D.C. policy makers and telecom executives, are likely to program racial injustice into 21st-century life.

There are, in essence, two Internets emerging in the United States. The first is the one that's driven innovation and commerce for the past two decades: traditional Internet hookups that connect wires to desktop computers and allow users to work, play and explore from the comfort of their home. That Internet is regulated—loosely, but regulated—by the federal government, which has issued rules that prohibit Internet service providers from interfering with their users' online access. Those rules exist as an implicit acknowledgement that the Internet isn't just fun and games, but rather the central communication platform of the 21st century, an essential medium for everything from commerce to elections.

Meanwhile, mobile wireless is quickly taking shape as a second Internet, one in which people of color and users with little income are entirely dependent upon cell phone companies for access. That Internet is unregulated. Companies are free to do as they please with customers—they can control what users see, do and say online. And as the country grows more dependent on high-speed Internet, the handful of companies who own its mobile version are steadily working to consolidate their power. Whether and how policy makers allow that to happen may determine who gets a voice in our 21st-century economy, and who's left as its prey.

America Online—and Mobile

Gaining access to the Internet is fast becoming a prerequisite for participating in civic and economic life. From education to politics to even basic tasks like renewing a license plate, the town square is increasingly virtual.

Take, for instance, the 14 million people out of work right now. Several large retailers require people to fill out job applications online. Home Depot, Target, Walgreens and Walmart— live companies that employ a combined 2.3 million workers in the U.S.—take applications online only. And while those 14 million job seekers are online applying for work, they'll be wise to surf over to their state unemployment insurance office as well. As more state workers are laid off, applicants for unemployment insurance are faced with longer waits and diminished support for paper applications.

The same goes for civic life. During the 2008 presidential election, then candidate Barack Obama was widely celebrated for his campaign's innovations in online organizing. The campaign aggressively targeted voters between the ages of 18 and 29 on Facebook, and even built its own online social network to aid supporters in their efforts to get out the vote. In 2011, the president launched his reelection campaign with an online video and e-mail to supporters titled, "It Begins with Us."

While television continues to be king in election messaging, the power of mobile political users continues to grow. A quarter of all Americans used their cell phones to connect to the 2010 congressional elections, according to Pew. That number is colored by race: While 25 percent of white mobile subscribers used their cell phones for political activities, 36 percent of black mobile subscribers used their phones to do things like tell others they had voted and keep up with election news.

For years, the gap between those who are connected to this electronic town hall and those who aren't has been a hot topic. According to the Federal Communications Commission's [FCC's] 2010 National Broadband Plan, half of all Latinos in the U.S. don't have access to broadband Internet at home, while over 40 percent of African Americans are without high-speed Internet in their homes.

Wireless Companies Interfering with Content

But as people of color have closed that divide with their mobile devices, they've moved into another uncertain realm. Already, examples of wireless companies interfering with content on their network are mounting.

Verizon customers, for instance, learned the hard way in 2007 that they're not in control of the content on their cell phones. NARAL Pro-Choice America, like many political candidates and advocacy groups, decided that year that text messaging was an effective tool to communicate with people who care about abortion rights. But Verizon disagreed—and decided its users wouldn't receive NARAL's texts. The company said that it had the right to block what it deemed "controversial or unsavory" messages.

"Our internal policy is in fact neutral on the position," Verizon spokesperson Jeffrey Nelson told the *New York Times,* in a rather confusing bit of Big Brother speak. "It is the topic itself [abortion] that has been on our list."

The uproar around that incident brought to the forefront an important question: Should the information that travels along our networks in fact be "neutral," or can Internet service providers have a say in the content that's available to their customers? The question of "network neutrality," as it is known, grew increasingly urgent.

The Obama administration's answer to that question took effect on Nov. 20. That's when the FCC's net neutrality rules officially became law. The rules, established after years of contentious debate, created two separate, but unequal Internets. They do prevent telecom companies from playing favorites on the Internet—but only while users surf the web on *broadband* connections. So in that part of the Internet, defined by how users connect to it, service providers like Verizon, AT&T and Comcast aren't allowed to block content or create special Internet "fast lanes" for users with money to buy entry to them.

But in the other part of the Internet, in which users connect via mobile devices, the FCC is ominously silent. It's an important oversight: As the Internet service market moves rapidly toward mobile phone networks, led by communities of color and those without resources to get broadband, there's nothing to stop the companies that own those networks from doing whatever they please to either users or content. It may have been in bad taste for Verizon to block messages from NARAL back in 2007, but there's no law against it.

The FCC's net neutrality decision was widely understood as a classic Obama administration compromise. But something more lurks underneath it. As the debate has continued to rage, the federal government has found itself in a far from ideal position to wield authority. Decades of deregulation in the telecommunications market has eroded federal power over the industry, even as telecom companies have built up extraordinary power of their own.

Pulling the Plug on Regulation

To untangle how today's phone companies became so powerful, it's important to understand what happened in 1968. It was, of course, a turbulent year. America was being pushed into new social and economic terrain, and many people weren't very happy about it. But it was a good year for one man: Thomas Carter, an independent inventor from Texas.

In the mid 1950s, Carter had begun to sell small devices that allowed people to attach two-way radio transmitters to their telephones. The machines were called "Carterfones" and weren't all that popular; between 1955 and 1966, only about 3,500 were sold worldwide. Carter had one big problem: AT&T's monopoly. FCC Tariff Number 132 outlined that "no equipment, apparatus, circuit, or device not furnished by the telephone company shall be attached to or connected with the facilities furnished by the phone company."

Carter took AT&T to court for antitrust violations, arguing that the company shouldn't have a legal right to tell people which devices they could use on their own phones. On June 26, 1968, he won.

The . . . decision paved the way for answering and fax machines to enter America's homes and businesses, but the broader implications were much larger: The tide was slowly turning against America's phone monopoly. Across industries, new players wanted to compete in the telecom game. Just a few years later, another ambitious entrepreneur named Bill McGowan sued AT&T for antitrust violations as well, arguing that the company was unfairly keeping competitors out of the market. In the fall of 1974, shortly after former president Richard Nixon resigned from office, Gerald Ford's Justice Department joined McGowan's suit, as the parties fought bitterly in federal court for almost a decade.

In 1982, *United States v. AT&T* was finally settled. The company agreed to divest its local operating systems in exchange for the chance to go into the computer business. AT&T chair Charlie Brown had as early as the mid-1970s seen the future of communication; it was to be in what he called the "information age."

The [President Ronald] Reagan administration, meanwhile, saw another future—one defined by deregulated markets. One by one, the government relinquished its watchful eye over industries, including airlines, railroads, banking—and telephones. Industry, according to Reagan's line of thought, would flourish if the government simply left it alone and let it work its magic. The game had indeed gotten more players, but there was no longer a referee to ensure that they played fairly.

AT&T's local operating companies, known as "Baby Bells," split off largely according to geographic region. But over the years, they amassed their own power. Bell Atlantic, for example, eventually morphed into Verizon. Southwestern Bell Corporation went on to purchase several of the other regional operations, and eventually bought its former parent company, AT&T Corporation, in 2005.

Just as Brown had promised, these new telecom companies plunged into the computer business. Mobile phones were the result. But unlike landline telephones, there is no "Carterfone" agreement insuring that mobile phone companies play fairly with one another—or their customers.

In 2001, a Republican-led Federal Communications Commission made that challenge many times greater by divesting itself of power over what is increasingly the core function of mobile phones. In a crucial decision, the FCC classified broadband Internet as an information service, instead of a communications necessity. That means that in the government's eyes, how and if people access the Internet is merely a matter of luxury. Telecom companies and their supporters now use that ruling to argue for the freedom that they enjoy in the wireless market.

"I think that what we see going on at the FCC is no different than what we see going on across the country," says Amalia Deloney, policy director at the Center for Media Justice, a progressive media policy think tank based in Oakland, Calif. "We're in a political moment where anything that's perceived as being 'big government' is trouble."

Still, for most of the country, all of this is just wonkish political machination. We have phones. They work. And they seem to get fancier by the day. We call or text whomever we please, and generally say whatever we want. The decisions our cell phone carriers make behind closed doors don't seem to matter all that much as long as we have the freedom to be heard. Problem is, that freedom is increasingly imagined, particularly for communities of color who are stuck in the wireless side of the Internet.

It's a sad and seldom discussed truth of our information age. Sure, there's a ton of information out there, but it remains out of reach to many of the communities that need it the most. And even when it is available, the companies that earn billions of dollars in profits from it also can dictate what gets seen.

Cyber Ghettos

Though we marvel at the latest iPhone or gawk at the speed of our new tablets, the truth is that most of our gadgetry is merely sugarcoated over a set of decaying teeth. Those teeth are the Internet: a stunningly complex, yet remarkably physical thing that's failing those who need it most.

Only 60 percent of households in America use broadband Internet service, according to a 2011 report from the Department of Commerce. Sometimes, it's too costly. But in other instances, services just aren't available or the infrastructure simply does not exist. Take Philadelphia. Comcast purports to offer complete broadband coverage to the metro area, but a 2010 focus group of local residents said that it doesn't offer service to the city's 81,000 public housing residents. Those residents have the option of choosing Verizon's DSL service. But to do so they would also have to agree to the company's phone package [digital subscriber line], which costs upwards of $100 each month.

The U.S. ranked a dismal 16th globally in the International Telecommunication Union's 2006 evaluation of countries' efforts to connect households to broadband Internet. By 2009, a similar survey by Strategy Analytics found that the U.S. had fallen to 20th. South Korea topped the list, with 95 percent of its households having access to broadband. Even those who are connected in the U.S. link up to a broadband that is slower than in countries with comparable economies. The FCC released data in 2010 that concluded actual broadband speeds in the U.S. are typically about half of the "up to" speeds that companies advertise.

Three Approaches to Fixing Broadband

Everyone agrees that America's broadband infrastructure is badly in need of an upgrade. But there are at least three distinct approaches to fixing it—one from the federal government, another from the telecom companies and yet another from advocates of the consumers who are caught in the middle.

President Obama has rested his legacy, rhetorically at least, on the country's ability to get its act together on broadband. In his 2011 State of the Union address, the president outlined his administration's ambitions when he said that the country is at a "Sputnik moment."

In the president's eyes, innovations in technology can be the economic driver that the country desperately needs. He emphasized that the goal of widespread high-speed Internet is about much more than relieving pressure on cell networks. "It's about a firefighter who can download the design of a burning building onto a handheld device; a student who can take classes with a digital textbook; or a patient who can have face-to-face video chats with her doctor."

So far, Obama's plan for creating that tech Utopia has turned largely on selling public utilities to private companies. In February 2011, Obama released a budget proposal that called for the sale of wireless airwaves. The sales would generate an estimated $27.8 billion, $5 billion of which would go toward the development of a 4G [referring to the fourth generation of mobile communications standards for cell phones] wireless network in rural areas.

Industry's vision, on the other hand, focuses on the idea that consolidation and deregulation are the keys to the future. Both AT&T and Verizon have come out strongly in opposition to the FCC's net neutrality rules, weak though they may be. In 2009, the company sent a memo to employees asking them to oppose the FCC's efforts. According to the letter, the commission was "poised to regulate the Internet in a manner that would drive up consumer prices."

Both AT&T and Verizon sued the FCC to prevent the rules from going into effect, arguing that they would stifle innovation. The industry believes that it needs more power to fix the country's wireless problems, not less.

Last March, AT&T took this argument a step further than even its few remaining competitors, when the company announced its bid to acquire T-Mobile. The proposed $39 billion deal would further shrink the already tiny market of cell phone service providers in the U.S. But AT&T argues that the merger is a necessary step toward improving the national broadband network. The company recently withdrew its merger application, after widespread public criticism, a lawsuit from the Justice Department and skepticism from the FCC itself. But AT&T has vowed to forge ahead eventually.

In many ways, AT&T finds itself in a strangely familiar position. Back in 1968, when the government's "Carterfone" ruling helped usher in a new era of industry competition, AT&T was also dealing with customer complaints of poor service. The difference is that four decades ago, lawmakers were slowly inching away from the idea that one telephone company could adequately deliver communication service to an entire country. Today, the fight is to decide whether two companies—AT&T and Verizon—should own 80 percent of the wireless market.

Big Telecom's Long Influence

If there's been one constant in the telecom industry, it's the extraordinary influence companies have in Washington.

They're D.C.'s most truly bipartisan, nonideological lobbying force, spreading their money around everywhere from the halls of Congress to the advocacy organizations that represent communities' interests there. Last spring, it was widely reported that AT&T's charitable arm, the AT&T Foundation, gave large donations to several high-profile civil rights groups. Those donations were scrutinized after several of the same groups gave vocal support to AT&T's T-Mobile bid and opposed net neutrality regulations. The groups agreed with the industry's approach to fixing the digital divide: Leave telecom alone, let it consolidate and it'll be well positioned to connect everybody to broadband.

In 2009, the NAACP [National Association for the Advancement of Colored People] received a $1 million donation from AT&T, along with another million dollars from the Verizon Foundation and $300,000 from Sprint, according to tax returns. The National Urban League received $500,000 from AT&T in 2009, along with another $250,000 from Verizon and $250,000 from Sprint. GLAAD [Gay & Lesbian Alliance Against Defamation], which later rescinded its endorsement for AT&T's merger, got $50,000 from AT&T.

The Communications Workers of America is one of the nation's largest industrial unions, representing over 40,000 workers at AT&T and another 35,000 at Verizon. It also eagerly offered up its support for the AT&T merger, in 23 pages of reply comments submitted to the FCC in June.

All of these organizations defend their support of the merger and decry the insinuation that they've somehow been compromised by the industry's donations. "We need to argue the merits of the issue—what works, what doesn't work—rather than attack groups who make the arguments," Lillian Rodríguez López, president of the Hispanic Federation, told me last June. The Hispanic Federation submitted a letter with 14 other Latino advocacy organizations in support of the merger.

Meanwhile, comparatively little attention has been paid to the vast reach of telecom companies' money into the American political system as a whole. AT&T has given generously to federal-level politics over the past two decades. In a list of top corporate donors compiled by OpenSecrets.org, AT&T ranks second, with $47 million in donations since 1989, while Verizon comes in at 34th, with over $20 million. Time Warner makes the list in 33rd place with over $20 million in donations.

The House Subcommittee on Communications and Technology has a total of 28 members; all but four have gotten campaign donations of at least $1,000 from either—often both—AT&T or Verizon. In June 2011, 76 House Democrats signed a letter endorsing the AT&T deal. The plan, they wrote, would help realize President Obama's vision for broadband adoption. All but five of them had previously received donations from the company. Twenty-nine of the signees were black or Latino politicians who represent districts that are predominately of color, and in many cases poorly connected.

For media justice advocates, all of this money has crowded out the most important voices for success in the president's Sputnik moment.

"We want a communications medium that's more transparent so we can control how we communicate," says Joshua Breitbart, director of field operations for New America Foundation's Open Technology Initiative. Breitbart advocates for a multi-issue approach that improves both literacy and access among consumers. "Right now we have an Internet that works for half the country, and we need those people who it doesn't work for to design a new system."

"A combination of smartphones, business software and microfinance may make the women's lot a little less hard."

Smartphones Give Rural Africans Access to the Greater Economy

The Economist

The Economist *is a weekly news and international affairs publication based in the United Kingdom. In the following viewpoint, the author claims that smartphones enable rural Africans to transform and modernize how they make a living. According to the* Economist, *handheld mobile devices have helped Ghanaian women who gather shea nuts to better track their goods, oversee and increase their profits, and gain new training in production and business. The smartphone project has allowed these women to form a federation of groups to enhance their supply as well as give them more bargaining power and opportunities with buyers, the author concludes.*

As you read, consider the following questions:

1. How do the women specifically use smartphones for selling their shea nuts, as described by the *Economist?*

2. According to the *Economist*, what is one big benefit of smartphones for the women selling shea nuts?

3. What types of training have the women received with their smartphones, as told in the viewpoint?

Abraham Takura leans over a jute sack and holds his Motorola smartphone in front of a white label, on which are printed a bit of text and a few black lines. It is not that Mr Takura has a penchant for dull photographs: The lines are a bar code, which he is scanning. His phone duly records important data and sends them to a server in the German town of Walldorf: This sack of shea nuts, belonging to Fati Karimu, from Chamera Fong, has been delivered to the warehouse in Janga.

Janga, in northern Ghana, home to about 3,000 people, is reached by a spine-jarring 40-minute ride along an unmade, red-earth road. Water has to be obtained from the pump, but telecommunications are on tap. A red-and-white steel tower, the ubiquitous sign of Africa's leap into the mobile-phone age, rises above the homes of mud and thatch, breeze-block and corrugated metal.

Janga's tower has been here for a few years at most. Its women have been gathering shea nuts from the bush for generations. It is hard, dangerous work: There are snakes in the grass and the nuts are collected after they fall. But they are an essential source of income. The nuts are dried and made into shea butter, of which most is used in confectionery and some in cosmetics. It is said to do wonders for dry skin.

Activity into Enterprise

A combination of smartphones, business software and microfinance may make the women's lot a little less hard. A similar, longer-running programme seems to be doing so for cashew farmers, most of them men, in the west of the country. The scheme is not simple philanthropy, though there is a good dose of that. SAP—the big German company that devised the smartphone app, makes the business software and hosts the server to which Mr Takura and the project's other field officers send their data—sees it as a commercial investment too.

In shea nuts, the software side of things works like this. Each woman is given labels with a personalised bar code. (Spares are used, with her name handwritten, if she runs out or a label rips.) She attaches one to each sack she fills, which typically weighs 85 kg [kilograms]. The smartphone scans the label on delivery and talks to the server again when the sacks are weighed and loaded onto a lorry. As a backup, paper trails are also kept. The software also records and reports what each woman should be paid, according to weight, basic price and quality; the buyer tests the nuts and pays a premium for the best. SAP's software can also break down a buyer's order, assigning bits of it to various groups of women. Carsten Friedland of SAP explains that the synchronisation of the data on the smartphone with that in the cloud does not necessarily require an Internet connection. It can also be done via bulk SMS [short message service], which will function with even the most basic mobile network.

In essence, this applies sophisticated enterprise software to a traditional—even pre-agricultural—activity, carried out by poor people in remote places. It is part of a broader effort by SAP and PlaNet Finance, an NGO [nongovernmental organisation], to turn that activity into an enterprise. The women used to work as individuals; they have now been formed into a federation of local groups called the Star Shea Network. This gives them more bargaining power with buyers and a brand. By working collectively, they can offer a surer supply, become more attractive to bigger buyers and cut out a few links in the market chain. In 2010, the project's first season, when there were 1,500 women in the scheme, Olam, a big trader and processor of commodities, bought the network's entire output of 93 tonnes. This year [in 2011] Wilmar, another big commodity group, is the buyer; the 3,000 women now taking part in several districts of northern Ghana are expected to sell it around 200 tonnes.

A big benefit is that the women have been able to sell their nuts later in the year, when they have dried more and fetch a higher price, rather than off-load them early because they need the cash. According to a study by Sonali Rammohan of Stanford University's Graduate School of Business, last year the women were paid 59% more for standard nuts than they would have got in the local market in June. For premium nuts, they gained 82%.

The women have been given some training too: how to produce better-quality nuts; how to act on price data received on mobile phones given to each group to check prices in the broader market; and how to move up the value chain into processing butter. This year around 50 tonnes of nuts (on top of what will be sold to Wilmar) are being turned into 17 tonnes of butter.

The Role of Microfinance

Now microfinance is coming into play. Loans provided by two local organisations, Grameen Ghana and Maata-N-Tudu, should allow women to buy gloves and boots for protection in the bush. (Last year Olam provided them as a loan in kind; this year PlaNet Finance has done the same.) The loans should also provide liquidity for the nut gatherers and working capital for butter processors to buy packaging material. The first disbursements of cash to gatherers and processors were made only in July.

Women in Janga say that they are glad of the protective gear and the phones, not to mention Shea Star Network T-shirts. They add that they are less scared of reptiles these days. Most important, perhaps, is their apparent confidence that no one's nuts will go unrecorded.

Why Current Smartphones in Africa Are Not Smart Enough

1. Short battery life.

2. Frequent screen breakages.

3. Irrelevant apps.

4. No built-in tutorials on how to use or set it up.

5. No tailored entertainment: Games are for a different culture and audience.

6. European models are preferred over the cheap counterfeit models that are always in disrepair.

Souleymane Camara,
"Mobile and Africa: Are Smartphones Really Smart?,"
Foolproof, December 2011. www.foulproof.co.uk.

Judging by the experience of cashew farmers at Wenchi, in the west, where SAP has been working with a group called the African Cashew Initiative, trust in the software and the accuracy of the data may be the key to the success of the whole venture. Officials from the local farmers' co-operative, which operates the scheme, say that farmers, seeing an electronic record of their produce, now trust their bookkeeping and believe they are paid what they are owed. The officials, in turn, are in a stronger position with buyers. Yahya Baro, the secretary who has overseen the scheme, reckons a lack of proper documentation has cost the union's members 15,000 cedis ($9,000) a year in its dealings with buyers. But traceability does not only ensure that individual farmers get their due. The union hopes that it will help it regain its fair trade status, which was suspended last year.

Stepping into the Formal Economy

Until now, the shea nuts project has been sustained by grants in cash and kind from SAP, the European Commission and some other sources. By the end of this year, SAP and PlaNet Finance plan to turn it into a "social business", taking it a stage closer to a commercial footing. SAP is making it an interest-free loan for three to five years; PlaNet Finance has secured money from the commission until the end of 2013. The idea is that women will see the benefit of being part of the network and pay a small fee out of their increased incomes to join. In return, they will have access to its various services, from loans to phones, and take a step into the formal economy, for instance by joining the national health insurance scheme. The two partners reckon the social business should break even within five years. Far-fetched? No more so than the notion, a few years ago, that a phone in Janga might connect instantly with a server in Germany.

Periodical and Internet Sources Bibliography

The following articles have been selected to supplement the diverse views presented in this chapter.

| Ken Banks | "Mobile Phones and the Digital Divide," *PC-World*, July 29, 2008. |

Clark Boyd — "Turning Dumbphones to Smartphones," BBC .com, April 6, 2012.

Killian Fox — "Africa's Mobile Economic Revolution," *Observer*, July 23, 2011.

John Hoffman — "To Address the Digital Divide, We Must Go Beyond the Headlines," *Nonprofit Quarterly*, April 18, 2012.

Cecilia Kang — "Kid Apps Explode on Smartphones and Tablets. But Are They Good for Your Children?," *Washington Post*, November 17, 2011.

Rob Roberts — "Digital Divide: Not Everyone Views Internet, Smartphones as Advances," LJWorld.com, June 17, 2012.

Anton Troianovski — "Can You Say 'WAH-wey'? Low-Cost Phones Find Niche," *Wall Street Journal*, January 12, 2011.

John Tullett — "The Rise and Rise of the Smartphone Elite," ITWeb.co.za, April 2, 2012.

Teddy Wayne — "A Smartphone Future? But Not Yet," *New York Times*, March 23, 2012.

OPPOSING
VIEWPOINTS®
SERIES

CHAPTER 3

Do Smartphones Have Privacy Risks?

Chapter Preface

From tweeting a vacation photo on Twitter to complaining about a coworker in a Facebook status update, people share more of their daily lives with their friends. The phenomenon has given rise to concerns of "over-sharing," in which too much personal information is revealed on the Internet and through social online networks. "As new technologies, devices, and services appear, everyone will continue to sort out how all of this will fit into our lives—and how we use these devices and services to connect with others," observes Genevieve Bell, director of user interaction and experience at Intel Labs. "It has become so much easier to share the small details of our lives with our friends and family, but I think some people are still figuring out the right balance between staying connected and 'over-sharing,'" she says.

Encouraging the urge to over-share, smartphones and popular apps allow users to capture experiences and express their thoughts in an instant and reveal their locations in real time. "People love smartphones because they take over-sharing to a new level," blogs Megan Butler for GSM Nation, a wireless retail company. But digital etiquette aside, smartphones complicate the protection of privacy. "Your smartphone hemorrhages information. And everyone is interested, even smartphone companies. Their policy is to store it, file it, and just generally keep it around for at least two years," she claims. "Everyone" includes strangers as well as authorities, Butler warns, citing a figure that Sprint, the nation's third-largest mobile carrier, received 500,000 subpoenas for subscriber data in 2011 alone. Additionally, Verizon received 260,000 subpoenas and AT&T 131,400 subpoenas that year.

In light of these numbers, some critics allege that regulation is lacking and law enforcement and government agencies have unfettered access to smartphone users' information. "The vast majority of law enforcement's demands that phone carriers and Internet services hand over users' private data don't require a warrant, and occur with little or no accountability," contends reporter Andy Greenberg, who covers data security and privacy for *Forbes*. "To paraphrase [former US secretary of defense] Donald Rumsfeld, we don't even know *what we don't know* about how much the government knows about us," Greenberg maintains. However, others insist that more personal responsibility be taken in over-sharing and using new digital technologies. "It's a violation of the ethical duty of self-care. We have an ethical obligation to protect our own privacy, no less than that of other people," asserts Anita Allen, a law and philosophy professor at the University of Pennsylvania Law School. In the following chapter, the authors address the challenges to privacy posed by smartphones.

> "The smartphones most of us now carry in our pockets can easily be turned into surveillance and tracking devices without impairing their primary functions."

Smartphones Have Privacy Risks

Timothy B. Lee

In the following viewpoint, Timothy B. Lee warns that smartphones threaten the privacy of users. With built-in cameras, microphones, and global positioning system (GPS) sensors, mobile devices can be used to track and monitor users without their knowledge, he maintains. Furthermore, cloud computing with smartphones, in which information is stored on remote servers, Lee contends, makes data more vulnerable to hackers, the government, and service providers. However, he explains that smartphone privacy can be protected in several ways, such as improving third-party storage, strengthening constitutional protection, and developing advanced data encryption. Lee writes about technology policy for Ars Technica, a technology information and news site.

As you read, consider the following questions:

1. What is the status of Fourth Amendment protections for online services, as described by Lee?

2. As suggested by Lee, how can privacy be protected with cameras and microphones on mobile devices?

3. Why are the privacy stakes higher today than in the 1990s, in Lee's view?

Around the turn of the century, the FBI [Federal Bureau of Investigation] was pursuing a case against a suspect—rumored to be Las Vegas strip-club tycoon Michael Galardi, though documents in the case are still sealed—when it hit upon a novel surveillance strategy.

The suspect owned a luxury car equipped with an OnStar-like system that allowed customers to "phone home" to the manufacturer for roadside assistance. The system included an eavesdropping mode designed to help the police recover the vehicle if it was stolen, but the FBI realized this same antitheft capability could also be used to spy on the vehicle's owner.

When the bureau asked the manufacturer for help, however, the firm (whose identity is still secret) objected. They said switching on the device's microphone would render its other functions—such as the ability to contact emergency personnel in case of an accident—inoperable. A federal appeals court sided with the company; ruling the company could not be compelled to transform its product into a surveillance device if doing so would interfere with a product's primary functionality.

The specifics of that 2003 ruling seem quaint today [in 2012]. The smartphones most of us now carry in our pockets can easily be turned into surveillance and tracking devices without impairing their primary functions. And that's not the only privacy risk created as we shift to a mobile, cloud-based computing world. The cloud services we use to synchronize data between our devices increase the risk of our private data falling prey to snooping by the government, by private hackers, or by the cloud service provider itself. And we're packing ever more private data onto our mobile devices, which can create big headaches if we leave a cell phone in a taxicab.

What to do about it? In this [viewpoint], we'll explore the new privacy threats being created as the world shifts to an increasingly mobile, multi-device computing paradigm. Luckily, there are steps both device makers and lawmakers can take to shore up privacy in the mobile computing age.

Cloudy with a Chance of Snooping

Law enforcement loves cloud computing. We don't know exactly how much information the government collects from online service providers, but Google alone fields thousands of requests from the US government each year for private customer data. Other providers have been less transparent, but they presumably experience similar request volumes.

Shifting data to a remote server makes life easier for mobile users, but it also makes life easier for people who want to access their data with or without permission. Data stored on third-party servers is much more vulnerable to surreptitious snooping not only by the government but also by hackers and the service provider itself.

Google's new privacy policy, which allows Google to more freely swap data among Google products, has attracted criticism from privacy groups such as the Electronic Privacy Information Center. Last year, Dropbox revealed it had accidentally left some of its users' data exposed to casual snooping for a few hours. Sony also had trouble safeguarding the data of PlayStation users.

A FreedomBox Future?

What can we do to avoid the privacy problems created by third-party storage? Ars Technica talked to Eben Moglen, a law professor at Columbia University and chairman of the Software Freedom Law Center. He argued the only way for users to truly safeguard their privacy is not to relinquish control of personal information in the first place.

The best approach, Moglen argued, is for "storage and sync service to be provided in a form which deliberately disables computation on that data on the storage provider." Under Moglen's preferred model, services like Amazon's S3 might help users store their data in encrypted form, but computation using unencrypted data would only occur on devices physically under the control of the data's owner.

Moglen is a driving force behind the FreedomBox, a project to build a user-friendly home server that would allow ordinary users to provide many of the computing and communications services currently offered by firms like Google and Facebook.

Moglen acknowledges it's a big technical challenge to make the FreedomBox a reality. Free web servers, mail servers, content management systems, and other software exists, but currently requires far too much user configuration to provide a plausible alternative to managed services for the average user. Improvements in reliability are also needed. And even federated social networking services like Identi.ca have failed to gain significant traction against centralized services like Twitter and Facebook.

But while progress has been relatively slow, Moglen believes his model will prevail eventually. "What we're talking about is what's going to affect the nature of humanity in the long run," he told us. "The important question is can we do it at all. We've never met a problem we can't solve"—given enough time.

Fixing the Third-Party Doctrine

While Moglen and his colleagues work on a user-friendly alternative to the cloud, users are entrusting a growing amount of information to cloud providers. Under a legal principle called the third-party doctrine, this data does not enjoy the

Then "Is someone spying on my phone?" Now "Is my phone spying on me?" Copyright 2011 by Yaakov Kirschen and Cagle Cartoons, Inc.

same robust Fourth Amendment protections available to data physically controlled by a user. That means that the government may be able to obtain access to your private Facebook posts and even the contents of your Dropbox folder without getting a warrant.

There have been some moves toward extending full Fourth Amendment protections to online services. In 2010, the United States Court of Appeals for the Sixth Circuit held that remotely stored e-mail is protected by the Fourth Amendment. And in January, Supreme Court justice [Sonia] Sotomayor called the third-party doctrine "ill-suited to the digital age." In the future, she may convince a majority of her colleagues to embrace the Sixth Circuit's arguments. For now, data stored in the cloud lacks full Fourth Amendment protections in most jurisdictions.

In the meantime, Congress could update federal privacy law to give cloud services stronger statutory protections than the constitutional minimum established by the courts. The last time Congress rewrote electronic privacy law was in 1986. Obviously, communication technologies have changed dramatically in the last quarter-century. The legal categories Congress established then don't necessarily make much sense today.

My Phone, the Spy

Lower Merion High School in suburban Philadelphia issued laptops to its 2300 students in the fall of 2009. Freshman Katarina Perich soon noticed the green light next to the camera on her school-issued MacBook was turning on for no apparent reason. "It was just really creepy," she told *USA Today.*

Perich's concerns were justified. The district eventually admitted it had installed an antitheft system that included the ability to remotely activate laptop cameras. The system had been activated and thousands of pictures of students' homes were taken and transmitted back to the district's servers. School district officials contend the surveillance was due to a technical glitch, and the authorities ultimately decided not to press charges. A civil lawsuit brought by some students was settled for $610,000.

A growing number of mobile devices have built-in cameras, microphones, and GPS [global positioning system] sensors. This means law enforcement agents no longer have to take the risk of physically invading a suspect's property to install a bug or tracking device. They can simply order whichever company is in charge of the target device's software to modify it to enable remote surveillance and tracking. And because most mobile devices do not have hardwired LED indicators like those on laptop cameras, the owners of these devices are none the wiser.

In repressive regimes, the danger of government spying is already considered severe. Removing batteries from cell phones is a common practice among dissidents. As the *Washington Post* reported last year, "The practice has become so routine that Western journalists sometimes begin meetings with Chinese dissidents by flashing their batteries—a knowing nod to the surveillance risk."

The Need for Notification

Chris Soghoian, a privacy researcher and fellow at the Open Society Foundations, argues all device manufacturers should follow the good example set by laptop cameras. A user-visible LED should be hardwired to every camera, microphone, or GPS sensor on every mobile device. Soghoian argues LEDs have become cheap enough in bulk that the cost of adding two or three LEDs to every mobile device would be trivial.

But LEDs cannot help against another, related privacy threat: the use of cellular tower records to track a device's location. This location tracking is inherent to the way cellular networks work; your cell phone provider needs to know which cell phone tower you're close to in order to deliver information to you. On the other hand, cell-site location data is much less precise than the location data collected by GPS sensors. The privacy risk is somewhat reduced.

As with so many aspects of privacy law, the rules for law enforcement access to cell-site location records have not been clearly established. Some courts have ruled the government can obtain this data without a warrant; others have disagreed. January's GPS tracking decision at the Supreme Court suggests that several justices are concerned about protecting location privacy, but the high court has not ruled clearly on whether cell-site location records are protected by the Fourth Amendment.

Crypto

We use our smartphones to send and receive e-mail, take photographs, store lists of contacts, access social networks, and much more. As our mobile devices become increasingly packed with personal information, the potential harms from losing our phones grow accordingly. . . .

There's a well-known solution to this problem: disk encryption. If the data on a mobile device were properly encrypted, then a lost or stolen device wouldn't create privacy problems. The new owner simply wouldn't be able to access the previous owner's data.

Unfortunately, full-disk encryption on mobile platforms is still a work in progress. One obstacle to effective disk encryption is the difficulty of entering a password with sufficient entropy using a touch-screen interface. On the desktop we commonly use passwords consisting of eight ASCII characters. But the "bandwidth" of our fingers is reduced on a touch screen, so smartphone password systems tend to be simpler, employing a 4-digit PIN [personal identification number] number or a sequence of simple "swipes." Yet these systems have few enough possible combinations—10,000 for a 4-digit PIN, for example—that an attacker can write software to simply try all possible combinations until he finds the right one.

Theoretically, mobile users could enter longer passwords. For example, a 14-digit number has about as much entropy as an 8-character alphanumeric password. But the average user is unlikely to have the patience to enter a 14-digit password every time she pulls out her cell phone. Soghoian tells Ars that finding more efficient ways to enter secure passwords using a touch screen is an "open research problem."

Still, Soghoian says smartphone vendors should at least offer their users the option to encrypt the storage on their mobile devices. Encryption with low-entropy passwords is better than no encryption at all, and users who particularly care about the privacy of their data do have the option of entering 14-digit passwords.

Making Privacy a Priority

This isn't the first time firms pioneering a new computing paradigm have failed to pay adequate attention to security and privacy. For example, it took several embarrassing malware incidents before Microsoft began taking desktop security more seriously. It may take a series of similar privacy disasters on mobile platforms before leading mobile vendors make security a top priority.

The stakes are higher today than they were in the 1990s. Users carry their phones with them everywhere, and use them for more purposes than they used their desktop computers for a decade ago. It would be a mistake to wait for disaster to strike before acting. Taking proactive steps now—like supporting full-disk encryption and adding LEDs to input devices—could avoid major embarrassment later.

Policy makers also have work to do. The Supreme Court should heed Justice Sotomayor's call to reconsider the third-party doctrine. And whether or not the court extends the Fourth Amendment to cloud services, Congress should overhaul electronic privacy law to ensure people enjoy the same robust privacy rights on 21st-century communications platforms as they do for 20th-century ones.

"These phones don't keep secrets. [Apps] are sharing this personal data widely and regularly."

Smartphone Apps Can Breach Privacy

Scott Thurm and Yukari Iwatani Kane

Scott Thurm is a senior editor for WSJ.com, the website for the Wall Street Journal. *Yukari Iwatani Kane is a staff reporter for the newspaper at the San Francisco, California, bureau. In the following viewpoint, Thurm and Kane contend that smartphone applications surreptitiously send detailed information about users, revealed in a* Wall Street Journal *investigation of 101 apps. According to the authors, fifty-six of the apps sent unique device identifiers without the consent or awareness of users, forty-seven sent the devices' locations, and five sent personal information such as age and gender. Furthermore, the authors insist that users cannot opt out of app tracking and many fail to provide written privacy policies. The data collected through apps is assembled into profiles of smartphone users and is used for targeted advertising, say Thurm and Kane.*

As you read, consider the following questions:

1. As alleged by the authors' investigation, what information did Pandora send to ad networks?

2. In what ways does Traffic Marketplace monitor smartphone users, as told in the viewpoint?

3. What types of information about people does Millennial Media list that developers can transmit, as described by the authors?

Few devices know more personal details about people than the smartphones in their pockets: phone numbers, current location, often the owner's real name—even a unique ID number that can never be changed or turned off.

These phones don't keep secrets. They are sharing this personal data widely and regularly, a *Wall Street Journal* investigation has found.

An examination of 101 popular smartphone "apps"— games and other software applications for iPhone and Android phones—showed that 56 transmitted the phone's unique device ID to other companies without users' awareness or consent. Forty-seven apps transmitted the phone's location in some way. Five sent age, gender and other personal details to outsiders.

The findings reveal the intrusive effort by online-tracking companies to gather personal data about people in order to flesh out detailed dossiers on them.

Among the apps tested, the iPhone apps transmitted more data than the apps on phones using Google Inc.'s Android operating system. Because of the test's size, it's not known if the pattern holds among the hundreds of thousands of apps available.

Apps sharing the most information included TextPlus 4, a popular iPhone app for text messaging. It sent the phone's unique ID number to eight ad companies and the phone's zip code, along with the user's age and gender, to two of them.

Both the Android and iPhone versions of Pandora, a popular music app, sent age, gender, location and phone identifiers to various ad networks. iPhone and Android versions of a game called Paper Toss—players try to throw paper wads into a trash can—each sent the phone's ID number to at least five ad companies. Grindr, an iPhone app for meeting gay men, sent gender, location and phone ID to three ad companies.

"In the world of mobile, there is no anonymity," says Michael Becker of the Mobile Marketing Association, an industry trade group. A cell phone is "always with us. It's always on."

iPhone maker Apple Inc. says it reviews each app before offering it to users. Both Apple and Google say they protect users by requiring apps to obtain permission before revealing certain kinds of information, such as location.

"We have created strong privacy protections for our customers, especially regarding location-based data," says Apple spokesman Tom Neumayr. "Privacy and trust are vitally important."

The Rules Can Be Bypassed

The *Journal* found that these rules can be skirted. One iPhone app, Pumpkin Maker (a pumpkin-carving game), transmits location to an ad network without asking permission. Apple declines to comment on whether the app violated its rules.

Smartphone users are all but powerless to limit the tracking. With few exceptions, app users can't "opt out" of phone tracking, as is possible, in limited form, on regular computers. On computers it is also possible to block or delete "cookies," which are tiny tracking files. These techniques generally don't work on cell phone apps.

The makers of TextPlus 4, Pandora and Grindr say the data they pass on to outside firms isn't linked to an individual's name. Personal details such as age and gender are volunteered by users, they say. The maker of Pumpkin Maker says he didn't know Apple required apps to seek user approval before transmitting location. The maker of Paper Toss didn't respond to requests for comment.

Many apps don't offer even a basic form of consumer protection: written privacy policies. Forty-five of the 101 apps didn't provide privacy policies on their websites or inside the apps at the time of testing. Neither Apple nor Google requires app privacy policies.

To expose the information being shared by smartphone apps, the *Journal* designed a system to intercept and record the data they transmit, then decoded the data stream. The research covered 50 iPhone apps and 50 on phones using Google's Android operating system.

The *Journal* also tested its own iPhone app; it didn't send information to outsiders. The *Journal* doesn't have an Android phone app.

Among all apps tested, the most widely shared detail was the unique ID number assigned to every phone. It is effectively a "supercookie," says Vishal Gurbuxani, co-founder of Mobclix Inc., an exchange for mobile advertisers.

On iPhones, this number is the "UDID," or unique device identifier. Android IDs go by other names. These IDs are set by phone makers, carriers or makers of the operating system, and typically can't be blocked or deleted.

"The great thing about mobile is you can't clear a UDID like you can a cookie," says Meghan O'Holleran of Traffic Marketplace, an Internet ad network that is expanding into mobile apps. "That's how we track everything."

Ms. O'Holleran says Traffic Marketplace, a unit of Epic Media Group, monitors smartphone users whenever it can. "We watch what apps you download, how frequently you use them, how much time you spend on them, how deep into the app you go," she says. She says the data is aggregated and not linked to an individual.

Big Stakes in the Ad Business

The main companies setting ground rules for app data gathering have big stakes in the ad business. The two most popular platforms for new U.S. smartphones are Apple's iPhone and Google's Android. Google and Apple also run the two biggest services, by revenue, for putting ads on mobile phones.

Apple and Google ad networks let advertisers target groups of users. Both companies say they don't track individuals based on the way they use apps.

Apple limits what can be installed on an iPhone by requiring iPhone apps to be offered exclusively through its App Store. Apple reviews those apps for function, offensiveness and other criteria.

Apple says iPhone apps "cannot transmit data about a user without obtaining the user's prior permission and providing the user with access to information about how and where the data will be used." Many apps tested by the *Journal* appeared to violate that rule, by sending a user's location to ad networks, without informing users. Apple declines to discuss how it interprets or enforces the policy.

Phones running Google's Android operating system are made by companies including Motorola Inc. and Samsung Electronics Co. Google doesn't review the apps, which can be downloaded from many vendors. Google says app makers "bear the responsibility for how they handle user information."

Google requires Android apps to notify users, before they download the app, of the data sources the app intends to access. Possible sources include the phone's camera, memory, contact list, and more than 100 others. If users don't like what a particular app wants to access, they can choose not to install the app, Google says.

"Our focus is making sure that users have control over what apps they install, and notice of what information the app accesses," a Google spokesman says.

Neither Apple nor Google requires apps to ask permission to access some forms of the device ID, or to send it to outsiders. When smartphone users let an app see their location, apps generally don't disclose if they will pass the location to ad companies.

Lack of standard practices means different companies treat the same information differently. For example, Apple says that, internally, it treats the iPhone's UDID as "personally identifiable information." That's because, Apple says, it can be combined with other personal details about people—such as names or e-mail addresses—that Apple has via the App Store or its iTunes music services. By contrast, Google and most app makers don't consider device IDs to be identifying information.

Assembling Data into User Profiles

A growing industry is assembling this data into profiles of cell phone users. Mobclix, the ad exchange, matches more than 25 ad networks with some 15,000 apps seeking advertisers. The Palo Alto, Calif., company collects phone IDs, encodes them (to obscure the number), and assigns them to interest categories based on what apps people download and how much time they spend using an app, among other factors.

By tracking a phone's location, Mobclix also makes a "best guess" of where a person lives, says Mr. [Vishal] Gurbuxani, the Mobclix executive. Mobclix then matches that location with spending and demographic data from Nielsen Co.

In roughly a quarter-second, Mobclix can place a user in one of 150 "segments" it offers to advertisers, from "green enthusiasts" to "soccer moms." For example, "die-hard gamers" are 15-to-25-year-old males with more than 20 apps on their phones who use an app for more than 20 minutes at a time.

Mobclix says its system is powerful, but that its categories are broad enough to not identify individuals. "It's about how you track people better," Mr. Gurbuxani says.

Some app makers have made changes in response to the findings. At least four app makers posted privacy policies after being contacted by the *Journal*, including Rovio Mobile Ltd., the Finnish company behind the popular game Angry Birds (in which birds battle egg-snatching pigs). A spokesman says Rovio had been working on the policy, and the *Journal* inquiry made it a good time to unveil it.

Free and paid versions of Angry Birds were tested on an iPhone. The apps sent the phone's UDID and location to the Chillingo unit of Electronic Arts Inc., which markets the games. Chillingo says it doesn't use the information for advertising and doesn't share it with outsiders.

The Growth of Apps

Apps have been around for years but burst into prominence when Apple opened its App Store in July 2008. Today, the App Store boasts more than 300,000 programs.

Other phone makers, including BlackBerry maker Research in Motion Ltd. and Nokia Corp., quickly built their own app stores. Google's Android Market, which opened later in 2008, has more than 100,000 apps. Market researcher Gartner Inc. estimates that worldwide app sales this year will total $6.7 billion.

Many developers offer apps for free, hoping to profit by selling ads inside the app. Noah Elkin of market researcher eMarketer says some people "are willing to tolerate advertising in apps to get something for free." Of the 101 apps tested, the paid apps generally sent less data to outsiders.

Ad sales on phones account for less than 5% of the $23 billion in annual Internet advertising. But spending on mobile ads is growing faster than the market overall.

Personal Data Collected by Pandora

The iPhone version of music app Pandora sent information to eight trackers. It sent location data to seven of these, a unique phone ID to three, and demographic data to two.

Data Being Sent	Companies Collecting the Data
User, password	
Contacts	
Age, gender	Google/DoubleClick
	Google/AdSense
Location	Apple/Quattro
	Google/DoubleClick
	Facebook
	Google/AdSense
	Google/Analytics
	WeeklyPlus
	Yahoo
Phone ID	Apple/Quattro
	Google/DoubleClick
	Medialets
Phone number	

TAKEN FROM: Scott Thurm and Yukari Iwatani Kane, "Your Apps Are Watching You," *Wall Street Journal*, December 17, 2010.

Central to this growth: the ad networks whose business is connecting advertisers with apps. Many ad networks offer software "kits" that automatically insert ads into an app. The kits also track where users spend time inside the app.

Some developers feel pressure to release more data about people. Max Binshtok, creator of the DailyHoroscope Android app, says ad-network executives encouraged him to transmit users' locations.

Mr. Binshtok says he declined because of privacy concerns. But ads targeted by location bring in two to five times as much money as untargeted ads, Mr. Binshtok says. "We are losing a lot of revenue."

Other apps transmitted more data. The Android app for social network site MySpace sent age and gender, along with a device ID, to Millennial Media, a big ad network.

In its software-kit instructions, Millennial Media lists 11 types of information about people that developers may transmit to "help Millennial provide more relevant ads." They include age, gender, income, ethnicity, sexual orientation and political views. In a retest with a more complete profile, MySpace also sent a user's income, ethnicity and parental status.

A spokesman says MySpace discloses in its privacy policy that it will share details from user profiles to help advertisers provide "more relevant ads." MySpace is a unit of News Corp., which publishes the *Journal*. Millennial did not respond to requests for comment on its software kit.

App makers transmitting data say it is anonymous to the outside firms that receive it. "There is no real-life I.D. here," says Joel Simkhai, CEO [chief executive officer] of Nearby Buddy Finder LLC, the maker of the Grindr app for gay men. "Because we are not tying [the information] to a name, I don't see an area of concern."

Scott Lahman, CEO of TextPlus 4 developer Gogii Inc., says his company "is dedicated to the privacy of our users. We do not share personally identifiable information or message content." A Pandora spokeswoman says, "We use listener data in accordance with our privacy policy," which discusses the app's data use, to deliver relevant advertising. When a user registers for the first time, the app asks for e-mail address, gender, birth year and zip code.

Google was the biggest data recipient in the tests. Its AdMob, AdSense, Analytics and DoubleClick units collectively heard from 38 of the 101 apps. Google, whose ad units operate on both iPhones and Android phones, says it doesn't mix data received by these units.

Google's main mobile-ad network is AdMob, which it bought this year [in 2010] for $750 million. AdMob lets advertisers target phone users by location, type of device and "demographic data," including gender or age group.

A Google spokesman says AdMob targets ads based on what it knows about the types of people who use an app, phone location, and profile information a user has submitted to the app. "No profile of the user, their device, where they've been or what apps they've downloaded, is created or stored," he says.

Targeting People More Closely

Apple operates its iAd Network only on the iPhone. Eighteen of the 51 iPhone apps sent information to Apple.

Apple targets ads to phone users based largely on what it knows about them through its App Store and iTunes music service. The targeting criteria can include the types of songs, videos and apps a person downloads, according to an Apple ad presentation reviewed by the *Journal*. The presentation named 103 targeting categories, including karaoke, Christian/gospel music, anime, business news, health apps, games and horror movies.

People familiar with iAd say Apple doesn't track what users do inside apps and offers advertisers broad categories of people, not specific individuals.

Apple has signaled that it has ideas for targeting people more closely. In a patent application filed this past May, Apple outlined a system for placing and pricing ads based on a person's "web history or search history" and "the contents of a media library." For example, home improvement advertisers might pay more to reach a person who downloaded do-it-yourself TV shows, the document says.

The patent application also lists another possible way to target people with ads: the contents of a friend's media library.

How would Apple learn who a cell phone user's friends are, and what kinds of media they prefer? The patent says

Apple could tap "known connections on one or more social networking websites" or "publicly available information or private databases describing purchasing decisions, brand preferences," and other data. In September, Apple introduced a social networking service within iTunes, called Ping, that lets users share music preferences with friends. Apple declined to comment.

Tech companies file patents on blue-sky concepts all the time, and it isn't clear whether Apple will follow through on these ideas. If it did, it would be an evolution for [the late] chief executive Steve Jobs, who has spoken out against intrusive tracking. At a tech conference in June, he complained about apps "that want to take a lot of your personal data and suck it up."

> "The smartphone privacy bottom line is the same one your mother taught you when you were growing up: Don't trust strangers (or strange companies, apps, or networks)."

10 Steps to Smartphone Privacy

Eric Zeman

In the following viewpoint, Eric Zeman suggests that smartphone users can use device settings and change their habits to protect their data and privacy. Zeman recommends that users secure their devices with a screen lock that is automatically enabled after nonuse and set up remote tracking and data wiping in case of loss or theft. To maintain privacy on smartphone apps, users should manage location settings to keep their whereabouts private; read the permissions to learn what types of data are being accessed, stored, or delivered; and to not download apps from unknown sources, he advises. The author is a columnist for In-formationWeek, a business technology magazine.

As you read, consider the following questions:

1. Why should smartphones system updates be frequently installed, as explained by Zeman?

2. As described by the author, what should the "permissions" screen let users know about applications?

3. How does smartphone data encryption protect privacy and information, according to Zeman?

Your smartphone is simultaneously your best friend and your worst enemy. It can help you find the nearest Starbucks for a caffeine fix, reach out to loved ones in times of need, or get the score of that vital play-off game. If it falls into the wrong hands, heck, even if it *doesn't* fall into the wrong hands, a smartphone can expose your contacts, location history, banking data, and more. Smartphone privacy was in the news again this week, due to a fresh Google and Apple iPhone privacy flap.

This all means smartphone owners need to be vigilant in order to protect themselves. Here are some essential tips to help keep your vital data under control.

1. Lock Your Phone

This may seem a simple and obvious step to take, but many people are too lazy to do it. Set up a screen lock so the phone can't be accessed or used without a password of some sort. Though four-number pins may foil street hoods, using a real alphanumeric password is much better. Make sure the screen locks automatically after 1 to 5 minutes of nonuse.

2. Use 'Find My iPhone' or Similar Services

It only takes a few moments to use today's smartphone tools to set up a free tracking/wiping service. Android, BlackBerry, iOS, and Windows Phone devices allow users to lock, track, or wipe their phones remotely if lost. Not only does this protect your data, it could help you recover a lost/stolen device. Do it.

3. Don't Leave Your Smartphone Unattended

Would you leave your Social Security card on a bar while you traipse off to use the bathroom? I didn't think so. Don't leave your phone sitting around in public where it can be grabbed by an opportunist. You may trust your coworkers in the meeting room, or friends you invite to your home, but don't be too quick to extend trust to people you don't know. Put it in your coat, pocket, desk (yes, even at the office), brief-case, purse, backpack, wherever. Keep it out of view.

4. Don't Give Your Phone to Strangers

That 'tourist' who needs to make an emergency call home and asks to use your phone? Dicey. It could certainly be some-one in legitimate need of help—or not. Rather than give the person your phone, make the call yourself, and put it on speakerphone.

5. Keep Your Smartphone Up-to-Date

You know that system update you've been ignoring for a couple of weeks? Install it. Nearly all smartphone system up-dates include enhancements to device security. Smartphone makers and carriers often ship phones with buggy software that contains loopholes that can be used to circumvent secu-rity. When updates are provided by the manufacturer, install them.

6. Manage Location Settings

Most phones come with either GPS or carrier-aided loca-tion tracking features. These are meant to enhance the func-tionality of applications such as Google Maps or Foursquare (after all, maps are kind of useless if you don't know where you are). Now, however, there are thousands of apps that want to access your location data, such as Google+, Facebook, Twitter, Instagram, and others. You can control location set-tings in these apps individually in most cases. If you want to make your location as secret as possible, turn off all forms of location assessment. This way, apps won't know where you are.

7. Do App Due Diligence

Speaking of apps, do your homework. If you value your privacy, read the "permissions" screen when you download and install apps. Many apps will let you know that they are accessing your location, call history, contacts, and other data. Be sure to note if that data is going to be stored by the app, delivered by the app to the app vendor, or sent to third-party companies for other uses. If you're suspect about the permissions, do some research, look online to see if the app has been reviewed by reputable sources, and so on. Also, if you download an app and stop using it, get rid of it. Don't leave it on your phone.

8. Don't Download Apps from Untrusted Sources

Most smartphone manufacturers only want you to download apps from their stores, but there are plenty of ways to circumvent this control. In Android smartphones, for example, you can choose to enable a setting that allows non-market apps to be installed. If you jailbreak our iPhone, you can install Cydia apps, etc. Don't do it. Apps that haven't been approved by an official app store are more likely to be invasive.

9. Watch Those Attachments!

Being able to access e-mail on my phone is vital, especially when I am traveling for work. Be careful, however, about opening the attachments sent to you by people you don't know. Take the same precautions on your smartphone that you would on your home computer. Same goes for downloads from web sites, social networks, shortened URLs etc.

10. Encrypt Smartphone Data

Today's smartphones make it relatively simple to encrypt the contents of the phone. This ensures that even if the phone does fall into the wrong hands and is accessed because the screen lock was bypassed, some level of protection remains. This is especially important for the memory cards of Android smartphones. The phone itself doesn't have to be stolen in order for you to lose all your documents, photos, songs, and other files.

The smartphone privacy bottom line is the same one your mother taught you when you were growing up: Don't trust strangers (or strange companies, apps, or networks).

> "While devices can be replaced, loss of control over the information kept on these devices can result in far greater consequences."

Lost Smartphones Pose Privacy and Security Risks

Scott Wright

In the following viewpoint, Scott Wright assesses the threats and risks to sensitive data and personal information on lost smartphones. According to his investigation, in which handsets were planted in metropolitan areas, there was more than an 80 percent chance of attempts to breach corporate data and/or networks. Furthermore, he continues, attempts to access photos, e-mails, and social network accounts were observed on more than 60 percent of the devices, but only 50 percent of the finders contacted the owners of the phones. Wright advises that companies and individuals take steps to protect their smartphones, given the significant potential for business losses and invasions of privacy. Based in Ottawa, Canada, the author is a security consultant, coach, and researcher.

As you read, consider the following questions:

1. In Wright's view, what are the personal consequences of a confidentiality breach of a personal or corporate smartphone?

2. Attempts to access online banking apps were seen with what percentage of lost smartphones, as observed by Wright?

3. If lost, why does an unmanaged, employee-owned smartphone pose a risk to sensitive corporate information, in the author's words?

In today's highly connected world, smartphones have become a key asset for individuals in everyday life, for both business and personal use. Their vast storage capability together with unprecedented computing power and Internet-connected applications make smartphones carried by employees a significant information asset that businesses must now include in their security plans. Furthermore, because smartphones are also a consumer item, individuals must consider the risks to their personal information stored and accessed using smartphones.

The theft or accidental loss of a smartphone can expose businesses and individuals to loss of any data stored on the device, as well as data residing in corporate systems or cloud applications to which the device might have direct connections. The use of consumer smartphones within a corporate environment further complicates the issue of data protection, as information may flow onto or through devices that are not fully controlled by the business.

Threats and Risks Facing Smartphones

The risks to information are determined by the likelihood and capability of threats, as well as weaknesses in protection of data, wherever it may be. In recent years, security researchers have conducted many studies and performed demonstrations on the weaknesses found in smartphone operating systems, as well as in the apps themselves. This type of research helps identify vulnerabilities that need to be strengthened in the devices and apps. While understanding and addressing these weaknesses is extremely important, it is difficult to know which of them are likely to be exploited without knowing more about the threats facing a mobile device in an everyday scenario.

In late 2011, Symantec commissioned Scott Wright of Security Perspectives Inc., to conduct a study in this area. Sprint also was a sponsor of the study. The Symantec Smartphone Honey Stick Project–North American Edition is designed to help businesses and individuals in understanding some of the most likely threats to smartphones and then associated information that arises when a smartphone is lost. A person finding a lost phone is defined as a human threat as opposed to a technical threat from attackers who use tools or techniques to attack a smartphone from a remote location via the Internet or via direct radio communications with the device from nearby.

The basic question answered is: "What types of information will the finder of a lost smartphone try to access, and how persistent will they be?"

By better understanding this type of human threat, businesses and individuals will be better able to choose appropriate safeguards in terms of policies, procedures, training and technology for employees using mobile devices. In today's world, both consumers and corporations need to be concerned with protecting sensitive information on these devices.

Scope and Setup

The scope of this study involved configuring 50 smartphones for deployment in New York City, Washington D.C., Los Angeles and the San Francisco Bay Area within the U.S., as well as Ottawa, Canada. The devices were intentionally lost in a number of different environments such as elevators, malls, food courts, public transit stops and other heavily trafficked, publicly accessible locations. As finders picked up each device and attempted to access apps and data on them, details of those events were centrally logged to produce a database of anonymous threat data that can be used by businesses when performing risk assessments on their information systems.

No security software or features (e.g., passwords) were enabled on any of the devices, in order to enable finders to initiate virtually any action without any complications. The objective in leaving devices unprotected was to observe what actions a human threat would take if there were no barriers to accessing any of the apps or information on a phone.

Aspects of Human Threats

The basic objectives of the study were to characterize the following aspects of human threats to a lost smartphone's data, and the corporate systems to which it might be connected:

- Likelihood of a finder attempting to access data on the smartphone

- Likelihood of a finder attempting to access corporate applications and data

- Likelihood of a finder attempting to access personal applications and data

- Likelihood of attempted access to particular types of apps

- Amount of time before a lost smartphone is moved or accessed

- Likelihood of a finder attempting to return a device to its owner

In the context of a lost smartphone, the human threat is simply an average person finding a lost device, with no apparent owner in sight. The finder may choose to either ignore the device, turn it in to a person or place of authority such as a store proprietor or a "lost and found," or they may try to access the device themselves. A person—either the finder or somebody to whom the finder has given the device—may try to access apps or data on the device for various reasons. Some of the logical reasons for accessing the apps or information on the device might be:

- They are trying to locate the owner so the device can be returned to them

- They are curious about what is on the device

- They are looking for information of value to them

- They want to use the device in the short term for free calls or Internet connectivity

- They are trying to reset the device so that it can be permanently reused or sold

Regardless of the motivation of the person accessing the phone, the fact that they may be accessing sensitive data should be a major concern to the device's owner, and possibly their employer.

A Major Concern for Employers

Believing that a finder is likely to return a lost device is potentially reassuring to a smartphone's owner, but if the finder attempts to access other information on the device, it could be considered a major security breach. For example, opening a corporate e-mail app might immediately give the holder of the phone access to confidential corporate information such as intellectual property, financial plans, bid pricing or personal information about employees. This type of confidentiality breach could cost the employer significantly in lost revenue opportunities or even legal actions.

From a personal point of view, such a confidentiality breach on a personal or corporate smartphone could result in major embarrassment, psychological stress or even extortion or discrimination, depending on the nature of information accessed.

If they have never lost a mobile device, many smartphone owners might focus on whether or not their device can be retrieved should it become lost. However, a smartphone owner may not realize that, even though the finder may offer to return the device, the likelihood of them accessing sensitive information on the phone may still be high.

Methodology of the Study

Each smartphone was loaded with a set of simple apps that had icons and names that would likely be recognizable to a finder. These simulated apps had no real functionality but were able to transmit simple event data to a central logging facility to indicate which app was activated and at what time. Typically, in most cases an error message or other plausible reason for the app to not work was displayed.

The data collected for apps on each device included:

- Device ID

- App name

- Time of app activation . . .

A GPS [global positioning system] tracking mechanism was also used to log each phone's position occasionally, which might aid in later analysis such as determining if a device was turned in to police, sold at a pawn shop, etc. The GPS mechanism was also used to determine if the device was still operating normally, even if no apps were accessed.

Note that on most smartphones, there is not an easily accessible file system as there is on personal computers. So, document type files less commonly appear on the home screens of most smartphones. Therefore, the majority of the icons on the devices leveraged for this study represented apps that initiate a program on the device. However, in an attempt to highlight corporate data during the study, files such as "HR Cases" and "HR Salaries" were represented on home screens with icons that looked like recognizable document types such as the PDF format or popular business- or productivity-oriented file types.

Measuring Intentional Access to Sensitive Information. Several apps had a simulated log-in page with a username and password prefilled to see if people would try clicking through the authentication of an app. This might be considered to be an unethical access attempt, since an explicit log-in page was presented to the user after clicking on the apps' icons.

There was one app titled "Contacts" which had only a small number of entries, including one entry that had the tag (Me) beside the name, so finders could easily identify the owner of the device. It included an e-mail address and phone number for the apparent owner of the smartphone.

Data Collection. Ten devices with fully charged batteries were dropped in each metropolitan area, all within a period of a few days. As log data was accumulated, it was stored in a database for analysis. Data was collected for each device for seven days, by which time most devices had stopped reporting data. When finders attempted to contact the owner by phone or e-mail, this fact was logged as well. . . .

Key Findings

1. *96 percent* of lost smartphones were *accessed* by the finders of the devices

2. *89 percent* of devices were accessed for *personal-related* apps and information

3. *83 percent* of devices were accessed for *corporate-related* apps and information

The Forty-Five-Second Cell Phone Scam

Be careful to whom you loan your cell phone. Here's the latest scam: Someone asks to borrow your phone to make a quick, urgent call. You think they are tapping out a phone number, but they are actually installing a malicious application (app) that allows them complete remote access to the contents of the phone, even after they've handed it back to you. The entire process takes about 45 seconds.

John Sileo,
"7 Simple Smartphone Privacy Tips,"
Deluxe for Business, February 2012.

4. *70 percent* of devices were accessed for both *business*- and *personal-related* apps and information

5. *50 percent* of smartphone finders *contacted the owner* and provided contact information

Corporate Data Is at Risk

When a business-connected mobile device is lost, there is more than an 80 percent chance an attempt will be made to breach corporate data and/or networks.

• A total of *83 percent* of the devices showed attempts to access *corporate-related* apps or data.

• Attempts to access a *corporate e-mail* client occurred on *45 percent* of the devices, which could potentially represent an attempt to contact the owner of the device, but still expose sensitive information.

- A file titled *"HR Salaries"* was accessed on *53 percent* of the phones and another titled *"HR Cases"* was accessed on *40 percent* of the devices.

- Attempted access to a *"Remote Admin"* app was recorded on *49 percent* of the devices.

This finding demonstrates the high risks posed by an unmanaged, lost smartphone to sensitive corporate information. It demonstrates the need for proper security policies and device/data management. This is especially true in the age of the consumerization of IT [information technology] and Bring Your Own Device (BYOD), when mobile devices are flowing into and out of corporate infrastructures at previously unheard of rates. If an unmanaged, employee-owned device is used for corporate access unbeknownst to the organization and that device is lost, the consequences of having no control over that device—for example, to remotely lock or wipe it—can be devastating.

Personal Privacy Is at Risk

People are naturally curious, but when a lost mobile device is discovered, curiosity can lead to the violation of personal privacy and the exposure of sensitive personal information.

- An attempt was made to access at least one of the various apps or files on nearly all—*96 percent*—of the devices.

- A total of *89 percent* of devices showed attempts to access *personal apps* or data.

- Attempts to access a *private photos* app occurred on *72 percent* of the devices.

- An attempt to access an *online banking* app was observed on *43 percent* of the devices.

- Access to *social networking* accounts and *personal e-mail* were each attempted on over *60 percent* of the devices.

- A "*Saved Passwords*" file was accessed on *57 percent* of the phones.

- *66 percent* of the devices showed attempts to *click through* the log-in or password reset screens (where a log-in page was presented with *username* and *password* fields that were prefilled, suggesting that the account could be accessed by simply clicking on the "log-in" button).

- There was an average time of *10.2 hours* before an access attempt was made; with a median time of *59 minutes* (based on actual access attempts).

These findings show how important it is for mobile device users to protect their privacy and sensitive information by using security tools, such as those featuring remote lock and wipe capabilities on their devices.

If a mobile device is lost, the owner has only a 50 percent chance of being notified by a finder that their smartphone was found. However, just because they offer to return the device does not mean they are not taking liberties with the owner's information.

- Of the 50 devices, the owner only received *25 offers to help*, despite the fact that the owner's phone number and e-mail address were clearly marked in the contacts app.

- *89 percent* of finders accessed personal information and *83 percent* accessed business information.

- *68 percent* of devices were *accessed prior to being moved* by the finder (32 percent were moved before being accessed).

- *5 percent* of devices were moved, but were not accessed during the 7 days of the study.

This finding highlights the fact that in many cases, regaining possession of a lost device may be a losing battle. But protecting the information on it does not have to be if the right precautions are taken. While devices can be replaced, loss of control over the information kept on these devices can result in far greater consequences.

> "Many courts have determined that em-
> ployers can effectively strip their em-
> ployees of any expectation of privacy in
> their employer-issued electronic equip-
> ment by issuing and communicating a
> policy that permits employer access to
> the equipment."

Employees May Not Have an Expectation of Privacy on Company Smartphones

William K. Pao, L. David Russell, and J.D. Weiss

*William K. Pao and L. David Russell are attorneys at Jenner &
Block LLP in Los Angeles, California, where J.D. Weiss is an associate in the litigation department. In the following viewpoint,
the authors state that employees may not have a right to privacy
when using company-issued smartphones. In reviewing a case
involving a police officer's privacy of pager messages, the US Supreme Court found that a search was reasonable, explain Pao,
Russell, and Weiss. This has provided some guidance to lower
courts in similar cases, the authors maintain, which have not
found that individuals have a reasonable expectation of privacy
on work phones.*

William K. Pao, L. David Russell, and J.D. Weiss, "Am I on Speaker? Privacy in the Age
of Smartphones," *Los Angeles Daily Journal*, December 16, 2011. Copyright © 2011 by
the Daily Journal Corporation.

As you read, consider the following questions:

1. What did the US Supreme Court reason in not finding that the police officer had a right to privacy with his pager messages, as explained by the authors?

2. As stated in the viewpoint, what did the US Supreme Court muse about the pervasiveness of cell phones?

3. What advice do the authors provide for employees enjoying the perks of work smartphones?

The recent explosion in the popularity of smartphones with their seemingly infinite applications, blazing speed, and ceaseless connectivity has revolutionized the way we communicate and connect with the world. Today, we not only use smartphones to call and text our family and friends, but to check our business e-mails, access social media websites like Twitter and Facebook, surf the Internet, watch movies, listen to music, manage our schedules (both work and personal), play games, take photographs, and shoot videos. And as the recent unveiling of the iPhone 4S featuring virtual assistant Siri demonstrates, consumers continue to embrace the newest available technology; four million units were sold in just three days.

Raising Serious Legal Concerns

Combining these separate facets of our lives onto a single device raises serious legal concerns. With their many uses and features, smartphones create and store a substantial amount of personal data. At the same time, courts have struggled with how to square decades-old privacy case law with this rapidly evolving and paradigm-changing technology. This struggle has only intensified as companies increasingly issue smartphones and other electronic equipment to their employees, blurring the distinction between public and private. Critically, when employees use employer-issued smartphones to manage all aspects of their lives not only their work-related affairs do they have reasonable expectations of privacy over their phones and content?

In the past, mobile phones had limited capabilities and therefore could store only a limited amount of data, e.g., telephone call logs and text messages. In contrast, smartphone users can now install countless numbers of "apps" and in the process create and store new types of data. Moreover, smartphones can collect information even when users are not actively "using" their phones. Perhaps most notably as we learned earlier this year [in 2011] iPhone users' locations were being tracked and recorded by their devices. In addition, it was recently disclosed that the Carrier IQ diagnostic software installed on most smartphones can record and retransmit a wealth of data, including web searches, keystrokes, texts, and location.

The availability of this data has already caused ripples in judicial proceedings. For instance, the new iPhone app Find My Friends discloses a user's location in real time to approved friends. One week after the app's launch, a man on the Mac Rumors.com chat forum claimed that he discovered his wife's infidelity by surreptitiously activating this app on her phone. The commenter added that he planned to use still "screen-capture" shots of his wife's location on the Find My Friends app in divorce proceedings. And as we saw in the Michael Jackson manslaughter trial, among the evidence the prosecutors presented against Conrad Murray were e-mails and conversations extracted from Murray's iPhone.

Guidance from the U.S. Supreme Court

With parties pushing the envelope, courts have done their best to address the legality of searching and admitting data culled from smartphones. In California, courts have examined this issue in the context of the Fourth Amendment and privacy protections under state law. While the outcomes have varied,

Employee Smartphones and GPS Tracking

- Some smartphones include GPS [global positioning system] capabilities that allow employers to track the whereabouts of their workers when they travel off-site

- Employers can use the GPS data to identify unauthorized activity that exposes the employer to liability or lost profits, such as speeding in company vehicles, moonlighting, dalliances, or inefficiency resulting in excess overtime

- Employees object to what they perceive as over-reaching, particularly where employers monitor employee movements during off-work hours

Anthony J. Oncidi, "Smartphones and the Law: Avoiding Legal Liabilities in the Workplace," Center for Competitive Management, March 1, 2011. www.c4cm.com.

courts have consistently emphasized the importance of employer-issued policies regarding electronic equipment they issue to employees. In fact, many courts have determined that employers can effectively strip their employees of any expectation of privacy in their employer-issued electronic equipment by issuing and communicating a policy that permits employer access to the equipment.

For instance, in *City of Ontario v. Quon*, the Central District of California and the 9th U.S. Circuit Court of Appeals determined that a police officer had a reasonable expectation of privacy in messages sent and received on a pager issued by the police department. Critically, while the police department maintained a formal policy giving it the right to audit pager messages, the department also informed officers that messages would not be audited if the officers paid for all overage charges. Reviewing this decision, the U.S. Supreme Court punted on whether the police officers held a reasonable expectation of privacy in the pager messages. Instead, the court mooted the issue by finding that the search was reasonable, making the search lawful even if the officers had a reasonable expectation of privacy in the messages. The court reasoned that the new technology at issue justified refraining from setting the parameters, perhaps prematurely, on an individual's reasonable expectation of privacy in personal data culled from employer-issued equipment, when a more narrow holding was sufficient. "The judiciary risks error by elaborating too fully on the Fourth Amendment implications of emerging technology before its role in society has become clear."

While reluctant to issue a broader holding, the court nonetheless offered guidance on the policy concerns that may ultimately dictate the evolution of this country's privacy laws. Critically, the court mused that the pervasiveness of cell phones may make "them to be essential means or necessary instruments for self-expression, even self-identification" which may "strengthen the case for an expectation of privacy." On the other hand, the low price of these devices might enable "employees who need cell phones or similar devices for personal matters [to] purchase and pay for their own." At least one district court has used *Quon's* limited holding as support for its explicit determination that "[a] person has a reasonable expectation of privacy in his or her personal cell phone, including call records and text messages."

Courts interpreting California law have been reluctant to find that employees have reasonable expectations of privacy in employer-issued equipment. Indeed, in one recent case, the Northern District of California noted that "[c]ourts generally refuse to find a reasonable expectation of privacy [under California law] in an employee's use of an employer's computers."

For instance, in *TBG Ins. Servs. Corp. v. Superior Court*, a former employee argued that he should not be compelled to produce a computer provided by his former employer for use at home. While "assum[ing] the existence of an abstract privacy interest in [the] financial and other personal information" stored on the computer, the court declined to find "a reasonable expectation of privacy in the circumstances." In making this finding, the court emphasized that the employer gave advance notice to the employee by maintaining a policy, signed by the employee, stating that the "communications transmitted by Company systems [were] not considered private" and were subject to monitoring by authorized personnel. The acknowledgement of this monitoring constituted the employee's "voluntar[y] waive[r]" of "whatever right of privacy he might otherwise have had[.]" Likewise, in *Sporer v. UAL Corp.*, the court found that an employee had no reasonable expectation of privacy in work e-mail. In *Sporer*, the employer had a formal policy of monitoring its employees' computer use which was disclosed and agreed to by its employees. The state appellate court recently came to a similar conclusion in *Holmes v. Petrovich Dev. Co.*, determining that a similar employer policy stripped away any reasonable expectation of privacy in a work e-mail account.

Still Evolving

In sum, much like the technology it is supposed to regulate, the law on privacy is still evolving and has yet to mature. But for now, employers seeking to draw clear boundaries should consider implementing and communicating policies that explicitly give them access to data on work-related equipment, including smartphones. Likewise, employees enjoying the perks of their new work phones should be aware of any company policies relating to their rights to those phones, lest they later be surprised that private and perhaps embarrassing (or, even worse, incriminating) information stored on their phones may be forcibly unveiled to their employers.

Periodical and Internet Sources Bibliography

The following articles have been selected to supplement the diverse views presented in this chapter.

John Brownlee	"This Creepy App Isn't Just Stalking Women Without Their Knowledge, It's a Wake-Up Call About Facebook Privacy," Cult of Mac, March 20, 2012.
Roger Cheng	"So You Want to Use Your iPhone for Work? Uh-oh," *Wall Street Journal*, April 24, 2011.
Preston Gralla, Al Sacco, and Ryan Faas	"Smartphone Apps: Is Your Privacy Protected?," *Computerworld*, July 7, 2011.
Eric Lichtblau	"Police Are Using Phone Tracking as a Routine Tool," *New York Times*, March 31, 2012.
Glenn Harlan Reynolds	"Smartphone Searches Not So Smart—Analysis," *Popular Mechanics*, April 22, 2011.
David Sarno	"There's Little Privacy in a Digital World," *Los Angeles Times*, October 1, 2011.
Matthew J. Schwartz	"Smartphone Invader Tracks Your Every Move," *InformationWeek*, November 16, 2011.
Natasha Singer	"Facial Recognition an Edgy Reality," *International Herald Tribune*, November 14, 2011.
Jon Thompson	"Smartphone Security: What You Need to Know," *PC Plus*, February 5, 2012.

OPPOSING
VIEWPOINTS®
SERIES

CHAPTER 4

What Is the Future of Smartphones?

Chapter Preface

Despite a lack of features such as optical zoom and manual controls, smartphones are becoming contenders as the "go-to" camera. According to the market research firm NPD Group, 27 percent of photos were taken with smartphones in 2011, jumping 10 percent from the previous year. Meanwhile, the use of point-and-shoot and other conventional cameras dropped from 52 percent to 44 percent in the same period. "For most people, the compromises are greatly overshadowed by the fact that a smartphone is always in their pocket and that it can share photos instantly," says Tim Moynihan, senior editor at *PCWorld*. "Those two factors are a one-two gut-punch to lower-priced compact cams."

In fact, the exploding popularity of photo apps—especially Instagram, which allows users to creatively edit their pictures on the spot and share them on social networks—can be credited for the rise of the smartphone camera. "The sharing and community is where Instagram shines. The app can seamlessly share photos with Facebook, Twitter, Flickr, Tumblr, and more so you can instantly get your photos out through all your channels," claims Ben Goodman, a video producer and photographer, in a 2012 *Business Insider* article. Furthermore, the gap in optical technology between smartphones and compact cameras is narrowing. Many of the top phones on the market in mid-2012—such as the iPhone 4S, Samsung Galaxy S III, and HTC One X—featured cameras that have eight megapixels, which were found on advanced point-and-shoot cameras about five years earlier. "[T]he camera on the iPhone 4S is capable of producing very high-quality images," Goodman insists. "The f/2.4 aperture enables the camera to work acceptably in dark situations and can even be used to create some natural 'depth of field' effect without a filter."

Not everyone is hailing the extinction of the compact camera, though. "Just because you leave the house every day with your cell phone and not a camera doesn't mean point-and-shoots are dead," says Joshua Goldman, a senior editor for CNET in an April 2012 article. He points out several advantages to stand-alone cameras, from shooting performance to better image quality to battery life. "After reading countless blog posts and comments about the death of the category, I can say for certain there are a lot of people who are completely unaware of what current compact cameras offer," Goldman insists. In the following chapter, the authors predict the future of the smartphone and how it will affect other technologies.

> "Seems unbelievable, but the same tech-
> nology that makes [smartphones] hot
> today will make them not tomorrow."

Smartphones Will Become Obsolete

Barbara Hudson

*In the following viewpoint, Barbara Hudson writes that the cur-
rent "must-have" smartphones will fall out of use in the next
two decades. She points out that people are relying far less on
phone numbers, further threatening the business model of the
telecommunications industry, which has previously failed with
fax machines and videophones. Instead, forecasts Hudson, people
in the future will wear video glasses that interact with all electronic devices and connect to data streams and the Internet. Furthermore, she asserts that telecommunications companies will
eventually fall and mainly supply wireless bandwidth. Hudson is
a computer programmer and technology writer.*

As you read, consider the following questions:

1. In Hudson's opinion, what other business model of the
   telecommunications industry is dying?

2. Why do phone subscribers currently keep the services, as claimed by Hudson?

3. What seamless experience will video glasses offer, as described by the author?

Smartphones and tablets might be the current hot technology, but history says it's all just another fad. Twenty years from now, almost nobody will own either device. Seems unbelievable, but the same technology that makes them hot today will make them not tomorrow. If this sounds ridiculous, consider what happened to another "must-have" technology that almost nobody uses anymore: the fax machine.

Back in 1991, the Baby Bells [regional telephone companies] were predicting an explosion of landlines and a corresponding shortage of phone numbers because "everyone will need a fax machine." Phone companies offered to lease fax machines for "only (US)$60 a month on a three-year contract." (Sound familiar?) Newspapers were offering early faxes of their main stories to subscribers for a buck a day. Every office-supply store had shelf after shelf of fax machines for home and office use.

All those dreams got trashed by the Internet and cheap computers. E-mail attachments killed the fax machine boom. Today a fax "machine" is a $1 chip in a laptop, and like the modem chip, nobody even bothers to configure it. Faxing the newspaper? Newspapers are dropping like old news, and paywalls are mostly money losers. Even those cries of "mom, we need a second line for the Internet" are just a dim memory. Instead of two, three or four landlines, many homes now have none. Indeed, many existing "landlines" are actually VoIP [voice over Internet protocol] phones.

Holding On for Dear Life

The problem facing the telcos [telephone companies] is that they're in the phone business, not the "find the best way for people to communicate and give it to them at a competitive price" business. Their product is access to the telephone network. Worse, their entire business model hinges on an archaism—the 10-digit phone number monopoly. People increasingly don't use phone numbers to contact each other, and the telcos are at risk of becoming just another data pipe for when you're not near a Wi-Fi connection.

Fax machines are just one of many examples of the future not turning out the way the telcos envisioned it. "Sure-thing" premium services like video calling never saw beyond limited use—too expensive, and people were not willing to shell out $600 for a videophone, plus the extra monthly charges—not when there was almost nobody to talk to on the phone network. Now it's too late. You can have your "videophone of the future" experience via Skype, Google Talk or Google+ hangouts at no extra charge.

Also dying is the business model of locking customers into long-term contracts by financing expensive mobile phones. Unlocked Android smartphones are going for less than $200 with no contract, and LG makes a nice $60 flip phone.

Rise of the Smart Network

Today the same technology that lets phone companies move voice calls cheaply over the Internet also directly competes with them. What keeps phone subscribers on the hook are inertia (the "phone number" habit), lower prices, and increasing services—all of which explain why I'm paying less for a phone with unlimited calling across the country today than I was for local service 20 years ago.

The clock is ticking ... and IPv6 [Internet protocol version 6] will be the second-to-last step in our journey to a phone-free future, where every device has its own unique "phone number" and the network has enough smarts to locate you wherever you are, routing all communications to the

nearest device, whether it's a TV, car, public security camera, or the active display on the shopping cart at the mall.

Smartphones and Tablets in 2031?

Let's go 20 years in the future. Pretty much every electronic device can interact with your video SPEKZ, which can be anything from a pair of plain-jane NokiaSofts to the latest cool shades from Apple. Cars, streetlight surveillance cams, water meters, televisions, and even your clock radio are all talking to each other—and your SPEKZ are piggybacking on their data streams. There's not a single laptop, desktop, smartphone or tablet computer in sight.

It's an amazingly seamless experience. The tiny twin cams on your SPEKZ let you share what you see with your friends and stream a copy to your home server. Your watch and charm bracelet contain sensors to detect your wrist movements and the muscles and tendons of your fingers flexing, all descended from Nintendo WiiMote technology.

Of course, since most men would be about as likely to wear a charm bracelet as they would a pink shirt (some things haven't changed), they can also sub-vocalize e-mails and use eye-tracking technology to make selections "just like a fighter pilot!" You type on your SPEKZ virtual keypad and pick from menus and icons floating in 3D before your eyes.

Passwords? "What's a password, mom?" Instead, your watch face contains a small camera that does both facial and fingerprint identification as well as other biometrics, and your SPEKZ do retinal, iris and voice ID.

It's a safer, more polite world. The latest Amber Alert system allows people to opt in to automatically search the last few minutes of their SPEKZ data stream against a possible match. Road rage is also much less frequent, and not only because most cars are driving themselves. People even stoop and scoop because other fed-up dog owners forward SPEKZ videos of the culprits caught in the act to the city and post them on the net.

SPEKZ systems are also saving lives. Before SPEKZ, 20 percent of all heart attacks went undetected. Now, biometric watchbands and ubiquitous Wi-Fi detect heart attacks, heat strokes and hypothermia earlier, and your SPEKZ alert medical services even when you can't.

How Do We Get from Here to There?

The telcos and ISPs [Internet service providers] will continue to try to oppose ubiquitous free Wi-Fi mesh networks, just like they're dragging their feet on implementing IPv6, but competition and public safety concerns will trump their increasingly weakened lobby.

With both phones and their phone network monopolies long gone, carriers will have to settle for being sellers of wireless bandwidth in areas without regular Wi-Fi coverage, and operators of commodity infrastructure.

> "The change that smartphones bring is computing power in the palm of our hands or in our pockets."

Smartphones Will Replace the Personal Computer

Charles Arthur

Charles Arthur is the technology editor for the Guardian. *In the following viewpoint, he argues that the technologically advancing smartphone will take the place of the personal computer (PC). Smartphones are now outselling PCs, Arthur says, performing what used to be the tasks of desktops and laptops: connecting to the Internet, using programs, and organizing daily life. Moreover, smartphones will be increasingly adopted in developing countries, where the costs of PCs are prohibitive and electricity is unreliable, he continues. The rise of mobile technology will impact the software company Microsoft, he argues, which dominates PCs but has not yet made significant inroads into the mobile market.*

As you read, consider the following questions:

1. Why do smartphones have an element of personalization and intimacy not seen before, in Arthur's view?

2. What does Tomi Ahonen predict about the price of smartphones for users in developing countries?

3. What is part of the reason why cheap smartphones are taking off in developing countries, according to the author?

When he was diagnosed with type 2 diabetes last summer [in 2010], Tim Smith was given a blood sugar monitor, and a notebook with a pencil. The monitor, obviously, to test his sugar levels; the notebook to note them down so he could tell his doctor.

Given his job in IT [information technology] for Sainsbury's, Smith wasn't about to use something so low-tech as pencil and paper. "I would have lost it or torn it," he says. A few years ago, he says, he probably would have taken the readings and entered them in an Excel spreadsheet on his PC [personal computer], to make pretty graphs.

But this was 2010, and so he turned to his smartphone, and quickly found an app—Glucose Buddy—that let him take his readings anywhere he liked. They'd be uploaded to the Internet, so he could access them any time. Graphs? Of course. Alarms to remind him to take a reading? If he wanted. Advice on diet? Available for a cheap upgrade to the free app.

A Huge Shift in Computing

Smith is just one of the millions of people around the world who now own a smartphone, and the number is growing rapidly. In the first three months of this year, just under half of all the 45m mobile phones sold in western Europe fell into that category—able to browse the web, send and receive e-mail, and run custom-written apps. That's as well as storing contacts and calendars, sending text messages and (how quaint) making phone calls. Worldwide, smartphones represent 24% of all mobiles sold worldwide between January and March—up from 15% a year before. The tipping point when they make up 50% may only be a year or so away. And before the end of the decade, every phone sold will be what we'd now call a smartphone.

Smith's use of his iPhone is typical of the way smartphones are used: to connect to the Internet, hold data, run programmes, organise our lives. They're fast replacing what we perhaps wrongly thought was an embedded part of our lives: the PC. Notice what Smith, an IT professional, didn't do: he didn't use a PC, and he didn't fire up Microsoft's Excel spreadsheet programme. That's indicative of a huge shift that's coming to computing, and was behind Microsoft's $8bn splurge in May when it bought the Skype Internet telephone service, and behind the rumours that Microsoft is going to buy Nokia, the Finnish company that makes the most mobile handsets and smartphones.

In this shift, there was an earthquake at the end of 2010. PCs had always sold far more than smartphones (which only date back to 2003 or so). In the first three months of 2010, 85m PCs were sold worldwide, compared with 55m smartphones. Optimistic analysts forecast that the crossover might happen in 2012. Instead, by the last three months of 2010, 94m PCs were sold—and 100m smartphones. Analysts believe that this trend will never reverse. (It continued in the first quarter of this year: 82m PCs, 100m smartphones.)

"Smartphones will keep growing in sales approaching the billion-plus levels of total handset sales before this decade is done," says Tomi Ahonen, a former Nokia executive who now has his own mobile industry consultancy. "The trend of PC sales is stagnant or at best modest growth, selling around 300m per year."

Microsoft is concerned about what is happening with mobile, because it knows it is the future, and threatens the two PC-based monopolies—Windows and Office—that have earned it billions over the past couple of decades.

Beyond What We Had Before

The change that smartphones bring is computing power in the palm of our hands or in our pockets. It is Internet connectivity almost anywhere on earth. That's going to have profound effects. Horace Dediu, another former Nokia executive who now runs the consultancy Asymco, says: "Besides being powerful, they're going to be ubiquitous. Not only in the hands of nearly every person on the planet, but also with them, or by them, all day long. They will be more popular than TVs and more intimate than wallets."

They're going to do far more than wallets (although they can already serve that function: a system called NFC, for near field communication, is being built into smartphones and will let you pay for small items with the press of a button). All the things you can now do with a smartphone would have seemed like science fiction only a decade ago: translate signs, translate words, take voice input and search the web, recognise a face, add another layer to reality showing you the quickest way to a tube or restaurant or the history of your immediate surroundings, show you where your friends are in real time, tell you what your friends think of a restaurant you're standing outside, show you where you are on a map, navigate you while you drive, contact the starship *Enterprise*. Well, perhaps not the last one. Even so, "A smartphone today would have been the most powerful computer in the world in 1985," observes Dediu. In fact, today's phones have about the same raw processing power as a laptop from 10 years ago. And every year they close the gap.

The element of personalisation and intimacy takes smartphones beyond what we've had before. Our mobile phone used just to be a repository of our phone contacts, some photos and texts. Now it's our e-mails as well, our photos, our Twitter and Facebook accounts (and, by proxy, friends), plus all those apps and games that we've downloaded to give it our own personal experience.

Yet ironically these new, more powerful phones are more not less disposable than the "feature phones" they are replacing. Ten years ago, if your phone was stolen, you faced a nightmarish fortnight trying to get your friends' numbers into your replacement phone's address book. As for the photos, videos, games and ringtones (remember ringtones? Record companies do, wistfully) you had stored? Gone forever.

Not so nowadays. The other week a friend had her iPhone stolen from her hand as she walked down the street. After a brief attempt to catch the thief, she wiped the phone remotely from her computer. Then she called her mobile carrier and reported the phone stolen. The next day she picked up a fresh one and installed all her old apps, e-mails, contacts and photos on it. Within a few hours, she was back at *status quo ante*. See if you can manage that if your PC is stolen or its hard drive dies.

Dramatic Effects in Developing Countries

Smartphones' really dramatic effect though will be on people in developing countries, where electricity supplies may be expensive or discontinuous, and the cost of a PC prohibitive, says Carolina Milanesi, who studies the mobile market for the research company Gartner. "Look at what a difference Internet cafes have made in developing countries. Now imagine everyone having that capability—surfing the web, having an e-mail address—in the palm of their hand." And even the thirstiest smartphone only needs charging once a day, and consumes less electricity than a PC. Says Ahonen: "The mass market consumer will increasingly find the smartphone is 'good enough' for most PC types of uses—similar to how the cameraphone was good enough to replace most cheap consumer cameras, and the clock on the phone replacing wristwatches, and so on."

Some might doubt the economic benefits of the smartphone in remote lands. But even normal mobiles can make a huge difference. For example, ocean fishermen in Africa discovered they could phone ahead to coastal markets to find the best prices for their catches. Imagine an app that fed that data directly to the phone: the benefits would multiply for a comparatively small extra cost. And that's before you start thinking about using them for health care. For Smith in the UK [United Kingdom], uploading his blood sugar levels is a convenience; in a country where medical help is a day's trek away, it could be a lifesaver.

For that reason, Milanesi suggests, PC penetration in those countries may never reach the levels it did in the West. You don't need a PC on your desktop when you have the equivalent in your hand. "People are still thinking that the 1.1bn smartphones that will be out there in 2015 will all cost $600 [£370]," she says. "But we'll get to 1.1bn because some of them will only cost $75 [£46]."

Or even less, suggests Ahonen: "If we take today's top phones with a 3.5in screen, 3G, Wi-Fi, 8-megapixel camera, full web browser—that kind of phone will cost $10 to sell profitably in 10 years. That means that anyone on the planet—even the poorest in Africa, Sri Lanka, Bangladesh, Bolivia, Paraguay etc.—if they can afford a $25 phone today, they can easily afford what we consider a top smartphone of today—and buy that as a new device—in far less than 10 years."

It's also much easier and cheaper to add Internet connectivity over a mobile network than to build physical telephone lines: Countries such as China and India with their vast and distributed populations have far more penetration of mobile systems than of fixed phone lines. That's part of the reason why smartphones—especially cheap ones based on Google's free Android mobile operating system, and made in their millions by "white box" firms—are taking off in those countries.

No Traction for Microsoft

And that's where Microsoft gets edgy. For most people in the West its name is synonymous with computing: Windows powers at least 95% of all PCs. For every PC sold, Microsoft's finances suggest it gets $56.50 in revenue, and makes $39.90 in profit—because once it's made one copy of Windows, it can make 100m for barely any extra cost. That's the joy of monopoly.

But on mobile phones, Microsoft hasn't been able to get any traction. Its new Windows Phone OS [operating system], launched in October, was on 1.6m handsets out of that 100m sold, less than 2%. Its Windows Mobile product sold more but is officially being shunted off into the shadows and hasn't been updated for two years.

Instead the dominant share belongs to Google, which gives Android away in return for providing its services—search, maps, access to apps in its "Market" (equivalent to Apple's App Store). It gets users for its search engine and adverts; mobile handset makers get a free, flexible product. Android now powers more than a third of all smartphones sold from various manufacturers, and the proportion is expected to keep rising. Google expects searches from mobile to exceed searches from PCs in 2013—though that might happen sooner.

Yet Nokia, which kicked off the smartphone business with its 9000 "Communicator" years ago, isn't thriving. The competition—from Apple at the high end and Android at the low end—is chewing up its business so badly that when Stephen Elop, a Canadian ex-Microsoft executive (previously in charge of the Office division), took over as chief executive in September, he decided that its software wasn't up to the job—and signed a huge deal to put Windows Phone on future Nokia smartphones. As part of the dowry, all those phones will use its Bing search engine; but it is to pay Nokia billions of dollars in return.

With the PC market showing early signs of a global slowdown, might this be Microsoft's salvation? The trouble is it might not yield much in the way of profits. Compared with that near-$40 in profit per PC, each Windows Phone handset licence generates about $15 revenue. Profits? Not really.

In that context, Microsoft's $8.5bn purchase of Skype looks like a plan to try to capture revenues from future smartphone users who already use the service to avoid high overseas phone call charges. The fact that the Skype purchase had strong support from Bill Gates, one of the technology's true visionaries who can see the landscape some distance off, means that is probably a big part of the plan. Compared with the money from putting Windows on PCs, the money from Skype and Windows Phone looks like slim pickings. But it might be all Microsoft is left with. There's no guarantee, after all, that giant companies will continue to be so.

A Little More Disconnected

What does Milanesi think the effect will be on society of the broader spread of smartphones? The analyst becomes less effusive and more reflective. "I think we're becoming worse at communicating with people because of these devices," she says. "Look around a restaurant or coffee bar at how many people, couples even, are sitting across from each other and they're both looking down at their mobiles."

Of course you'd never dream of getting your chunky laptop out in such circumstances. But because your smartphone is smaller, more personal, its promise of new information is more seductive. And so we use it.

"There's a part of this that's useful, where you get information where and when you need it—such as maps or prices," says Milanesi. "But then there's also the aspect where my eyes are constantly diverted by a little screen. And we lose that human side of ourselves, which I think is quite worrying."

It's a strange vision of a connected world where we're all a little more disconnected. One thing is certain though: We're all going to have one.

"Pulling a plastic card out of a leather billfold at a cash register will look as antiquated as an abacus."

Mobile Banking on Smartphones Will Replace Wallets

Jameson Berkow

In the following viewpoint, Jameson Berkow insists that the wallet—credit, debit, and loyalty cards, as well as money—will go digital and be replaced by smartphones. Berkow says that near field communication (NFC) allows devices to exchange data by tapping a sensor or through transmissions over short distances. With NFC, he explains, card information embedded in smartphones could be easily shared with a swipe at the register. Companies and wireless carriers are already preparing for the digital wallet in Canada, the author claims, as the use of cash has been in marked decline due to preferences for electronic transactions. Berkow is a reporter for the Financial Post, *the business section of the* National Post, *a Canadian newspaper.*

As you read, consider the following questions:

1. What items does the author compare to the smartphone's replacement of the physical wallet?

Jameson Berkow, "Smart (Phone) Money," *Financial Post*, April 23, 2011. Material reprinted with the express permission of National Post, a division of Postmedia Network Inc.

2. Why will the physical wallet never completely disappear, as stated by the author?

3. How is identification adapting to the digital wallet in Ontario, Canada, according to the author?

Everyone has watched demand for physical books, music albums and movies wane for years as consumers found e-books, MP3s and Internet videos to be cheaper and more conveniently accessible digital alternatives.

Pretty soon, the same will be said for your old leather friend—the wallet—and pretty much everything in it.

Near field communication (NFC) is the technology that will bring about the digital replacement of the centuries-old wallet, starting this year [2011]. By securely embedding all the information now found in the plethora of cards, cash and identification in a typical wallet directly onto a smartphone, NFC will eventually reduce the physical wallet to the status of historical relic.

"The whole ecosystem and the road map for NFC where it relates to payment is that very soon you'll get the kind of digital wallet where you can store your loyalty cards and the points that you accumulate will be automatically transferred the moment you make a purchase," said Nitesh Patel, senior analyst for the global wireless practice of Strategy Analytics.

Similar to the way credit and debit cards embedded with "smart chips" work today, NFC chips release payment or ID data when in contact with a compatible receiver. The difference is that unlike "smart chips," NFC chips needn't be attached to a tactile product of a given shape—such as a rectangular credit card—because they transmit data wirelessly over short distances.

That means NFC chips, loaded with everything one might need in a wallet, can be embedded directly within a smartphone. Widespread availability of NFC-enabled smartphones has been the only thing keeping the digital wallet from rising sooner.

But now, NFC chips are widely expected to be nestled at the core of the next generation of devices from leading mobile players like Apple Inc. and Research in Motion Ltd.

"We've been waiting for something to happen as an industry in Canada for many, many years," said Drazen Lalovic, vice president of wireless market planning for Telus Corp. "Finally I would say now we are hitting that inflection point."

Preparing for the Shift

Credit card companies like Visa and MasterCard have already been working on more limited contact-free payment methods using NFC for years and some—like MasterCard's PayPass feature—have proven to be quite popular among consumers.

MasterCard is already conducting trials to introduce a mobile app version of PayPass for NFC phones, which would eliminate the need to carry a credit card at all. Many major rewards providers—like the Starbucks Rewards program—already offer digital replacements for their physical cards in the form of mobile apps.

That just leaves debit cards, ID and petty cash inside the physical wallet; and they are next up on the digitization block.

Interac, Canada's largest processor of debit purchases, has been preparing for the shift to NFC since 2009. Its first contactless product—called Interac Flash—will provide a function similar to that of MasterCard's PayPass by allowing cardholders to tap their debit cards against a terminal to complete a purchase.

"NFC will become a mainstream payment method," said Allen Wright, vice president of product with the Interac Association. "These things take a fair amount of time, but any time you can bring a bunch of factors together such as convenience, utility, acceptance and security; if you can get those things together at the same point in time and deliver them to the consumer, it is almost like why wouldn't they use it?"

With the first Interac Flash–capable cards expected to become available to Bank of Nova Scotia and Royal Bank of Canada customers this summer, the payment provider has no intention of stopping there. Flash is the first stage in a much longer process, Mr. Wright explained.

"The second stage will be to take Flash and incorporate it into the mobile phone device, which is the NFC function," he said.

The target is to have a pilot program in place by next year. Once NFC phones reach a "critical mass" in the market, which Mr. Wright expects will happen in the next few years, Interac will be able to follow suit "within a three-to-five-year window."

As one of Canada's largest wireless carriers, Telus has also been working for years in tandem with financial institutions and other carriers to ensure its network can support what could quickly become millions of purchases made daily with a wireless device.

"We started seeing a few phones with cameras, then many phones with cameras, now every single phone has a camera," Mr. Lalovic said, comparing the rise of the smartphone camera to the smartphone wallet. "We should expect to see the same pattern with NFC capabilities on phones, but even more accelerated."

The Use of Cash in Decline

Meanwhile, the use of cash has been in rapid decline as consumers display an open preference for various electronic alternatives. The number of point-of-sale (POS) transactions made in Canada using debit cards in place of cash has been growing steadily since 2005, according to data from the Canadian Bankers Association.

Expanding Tourism

Mobile-wallet technology will expand tourism in developing countries by improving the ability to facilitate electronic transactions in locations that were once remote. Tourists ranging from high school backpackers to high-flying business executives will find this technology affordable and accessible. The technology will reduce the difficulty of handling and exchanging unfamiliar currency for travelers who are on trips involving a single or multiple destinations. Moreover, it will ease the difficulty of engaging local merchants who were previously unable to process electronic transactions. With the simple use of a mobile phone keypad, tourists will find it easier to transcend language barriers and unfamiliar currency to purchase goods and services from the smallest street vendors. This will allow the tourist to gain a better appreciation for the country of destination because it allows increased interaction with local merchants. At the same time, developing economies will get a boost from the ground up, as tourists will be empowered to explore the shops and stalls of countless small businesses and vendors in some of the most remote markets throughout the globe.

Jennifer Blanke and Thea Chiesa,
The Travel & Tourism Competitiveness Report 2007.
Geneva, Switzerland: World Economic Forum, 2007, p. 80.

That comes as no surprise to Mr. Patel of Strategy Analytics.

"There is already a trend away from handling cash," he said. "[The amount of cash that people carry on average] has been low and has continued to fall quite a lot over the last two to three years."

Ending any possible doubt that the way Canadians pay is in a state of dramatic transformation, federal minister of finance Jim Flaherty established a payment task force last June to ensure regulations keep pace with the changes.

"Today, Canadians can pay for things in a bewildering number of ways, even by tapping a cell phone against a scanner," Mr. Flaherty told an industry conference in Vancouver on June 18, 2010.

The physical wallet will never completely disappear. Just as with printed books and newspapers, many people will still prefer the tactile experience of a currency holder over the convenience of a digital alternative.

Those arguments will subside with the passage of time, Mr. Patel argues.

"I've always believed that people place strong value on physical media such as CDs and DVDs, but it has become abundantly clear that the younger age groups are quite happy to have things in digital format only," he said.

"That wave of youngsters is where we could eventually see the phasing out of things like wallets in the much longer term."

As credit, debit and rewards cards all fall by the digital wayside, one final vestige of the physical wallet remains: government-issued identification.

Yet even that is adapting to the digital times. It has been nearly two years since Ontario first introduced a new form of driver's licence with radio frequency identification (RFID) technology—virtually identical to NFC—directly embedded in the licence to allow for wireless scanning.

While that is still just an enhanced version of a physical card, it would seem to only be a matter of time before the embedded information becomes transferable.

Once that happens, pulling a plastic card out of a leather billfold at a cash register will look as antiquated as an abacus.

> *"Before most of us have even started using our smartphones to pay for things, the players . . . will spend a lot of money to make sure that they get to participate in the industry."*

The Format for Mobile Banking on Smartphones Is Uncertain

David W. Schropfer

David W. Schropfer is head of mobile commerce for the Luciano Group, a telecommunications development and advisory firm, and author of The SmartPhone Wallet: Understanding the Disruption Ahead. *In the following viewpoint excerpted from* The SmartPhone Wallet, *Schropfer claims that mobile banking on smartphones is headed toward a "format war," in which companies will compete for dominance. He persists, however, that the best or most innovative products may become casualties in this war. Most users are unwilling to switch to better formats because of the costs or inconvenience, Schropfer contends, determining which format survives in the next several years. Therefore, he advises consumers to be flexible and choose their smartphone wallet wisely.*

As you read, consider the following questions:

1. What does the author warn consumers about choosing inferior products based on marketing campaigns or what is easiest?

2. How do mobile payment and marketing companies make it less likely for users to switch, as stated by Schropfer?

3. What is one of the biggest lessons learned from the "Format Wars," in the author's opinion?

Logically, every system of payment that does not involve the current format, by definition, involves a "new" format. These are the companies that will allow you, for example, to make a purchase that is charged to your mobile phone bill instead of your credit card statement. Or, companies like PayPal that let you load your money into your virtual account and manage that money with more freedom and flexibility than you could out of a traditional checking or savings account.

And there are many other new ideas and products that focus specifically on a new format of completing payments using your smartphone.

So, these two formats are already beginning to conflict with one another. Before most of us have even started using our smartphones to pay for things, the players are lining up along each of these two formats, and they will spend a lot of money to make sure that they get to participate in the industry, and the other format will not get to participate.

Sounds a little bit like the start of the war, right? Well it is. And one thing that is true about all wars is that there are casualties. If you remember nothing else from this [viewpoint], remember that we, as consumers, need to make sure that the best products on the market do not become senseless casualties in a format war.

The Format War

Mobile commerce companies will present you with offers that are easy to join, and easy to use, but they will make it hard for you to switch to another company's product once you have joined.

It is called a "Format War." Two or more companies with different products compete for your attention. Of course, as a consumer, you get to choose the product you want. If you don't like it, certainly you are free to switch to another product. However, since companies know this, they can make it incredibly cumbersome for you to do so.

Now, just for a moment, look past all of the predictions that credit cards will disappear in a matter of months, and that the global economy will be changed forever, and that your whole wallet will become obsolete all because of the new technology called smartphone. Here's why it's important to take a moment and do this:

The next three to five years will determine the type of technology that most of us will end up using for at least the next decade.

Why?

Because one of the biggest components in a format war is the price of switching. If you make a choice to purchase one format versus the other, and it costs a lot of money when/if you realize you made a mistake, you're more likely to live with your mistake rather than incur a new cost associated with switching. The risk, of course, is that if the other format is truly superior and it does not get the support it needs to survive then that format may go away, and we all lose the advantages it offered. . . .

Apple vs. Microsoft

Although the competition between Apple and Microsoft continues as of 2010, the format war that took place between these two companies around the time of their origin and through the 1980s is a classic example of something consumers generally want to avoid: An inferior product beats a superior product so badly in the marketplace that the superior product vanishes entirely from the marketplace. Obviously, Apple did not disappear from the marketplace, but it came awfully close. . . .

It was not until Apple introduced the iMac almost 10 years later in 1998 that Apple began to return to profitability.

Windows had won the first round of the battle with its Windows 2.0 product built on the innovation of the Apple team. Think of what would have happened if Apple did not survive the difficult years between 1989 and 1998; there would be a host of products that would either be absent from the marketplace today, like the iPod, the iPhone, the iMac, and other popular Apple products all because we, the consumer— you and I—chose the Windows-based format instead of the Apple format.

At the time, nobody could have anticipated the contribution that Apple would make in later years, or how the Microsoft Windows 2.0 malfunctions and errors would continue for another 20 years. The marketplace was convinced, and hopeful because they had already spent their money, that Microsoft would figure out how to stabilize its operating system before the next version of Windows appeared.

If you purchased a computer in the late 80s, would you have chosen a Windows-based machine if you thought it would lead to the demise of one of the most innovative companies in history? Had you known about the superiority of Apple's modern products, would you have supported them in their infancy?

The answer to those questions is up to you, but the message is loud and clear. This is the choice you have right now for the smartphone wallet.

If you choose inferior products, and use services based on marketing campaigns, or what is easiest, and *not* through quality, you could be giving up a future line of products, money management tools, security features, convenience, and power that none of us can imagine today. As you hear more and more about the social and economic impact of new products that will be introduced over the next 20 years, remember this: These advancements really are possible, but they will be based on the market success of the products that you are introduced to over the next three to five years.

Difficult to Tell the Difference

As the saying goes: Those who do not know their history are bound to repeat it. Mobile payment and mobile marketing companies have always been laser focused on offering you a service that is easy to join, and free to join, but over time collects more data and more preferences and more patterns from you until it becomes an indispensible service to you. That is when you become less likely to switch to another company's service if the opportunity presents itself.

If you are flexible, and willing to try different solutions, then you do have more than one choice. But . . . most of us are not willing to try another solution—even if it may be better—if the time or expense of switching is too high.

As of the end of 2010, there are over 100 different companies with products that allow you to use your smartphone to either buy products, or get discounts at a retail store. Some are efficient and some are not. Some are based on very old technology and others rely on modern efficient equipment. Some will simply cost you more money to use over time than others. The problem is it is difficult to tell the difference. And, once you have made your selection, you are less likely to switch to another product. . . .

So, in an attempt to oversimplify the context, think of it this way: Smartphone technology will either be the next evolution of the payment system as we know it today, or it will change the payment system as we know it today.

Every product in the market fits into one of these two camps. The only question is which camp will provide the best services for you?

If enough people choose the most expensive solutions, from the biggest brands with the most marketing dollars to spend, then the new more efficient solutions may no longer be available.

Choose Wisely

You are about to change a big part of our economic system. Yes, you. How will you do that? With a vote.

This vote, however, does not have the luxury of being part of the political system. What I mean is this: When you cast a ballot for an elected official, the ballot box, or the voting booth, are dead giveaways that you are voting, right? But when you change our economic system, ... none of these companies are going to tell you that you are casting a ballot. And certainly, none of these companies will remind you that, like most things you vote for, you may have to live with your decision for a long time.

One of the biggest lessons learned in all the "Format Wars" described is that it caused many people to choose option "C." Meaning, they didn't choose at all. Millions of consumers chose to wait it out for one of the players to emerge victorious before they made an investment or commitment.

Periodical and Internet Sources Bibliography

The following articles have been selected to supplement the diverse views presented in this chapter.

Edward C. Baig	"When Will We Be Paying for Stuff with Our Smartphones?," *USA Today*, August 10, 2011.
Tim Bajarin	"Why the iPhone Has a Head Start on the Future of Personal Computing," *Time*, February 27, 2012.
Jeff Bertolucci	"Smartphone Sales Boom—Who Needs a Laptop?," *PCWorld*, February 4, 2012.
Fast Company	"Your Smartphone Will Soon Double as Your Wallet," September 2010.
David Lagesse	"How the Phone Is Replacing the Computer," *US News & World Report*, April 2, 2009.
Stew Magnuson	"Rise of Smartphones May Sound Death Knell for Old Push-to-Talk Radios," *National Defense*, January 2012.
John Naughton	"Real Cost of the Smartphone Revolution," *Observer*, June 2, 2012.
Matt Richtel and Verne G. Kopytoff	"Tools of Entry, No Need for a Key Chain," *New York Times*, July 3, 2011.
Joel Santo Domingo	"The Desktop PC Is Not Dead, Damn It!," *PC Magazine*, August 11, 2011.
Gentry Underwood	"Computer, Walk with Me," TechCrunch.com, August 5, 2012.

For Further Discussion

Chapter 1

1. Richard Fisher describes the numerous ways he depends on his smartphone and apps in his everyday life. In your opinion, does his reliance on technology simplify or complicate everyday activities? Explain using examples from the text.

2. Brian X. Chen insists that smartphones enable people to multitask. However, Joe Golton says that the devices are a major cause of interruptions in work and other activities. In your view, who offers the more persuasive argument? Provide examples from the viewpoints to support your answer.

3. The editors of *Maclean's* argue that smartphones are a major distraction in the classroom because they divert students' attention. In your opinion, does David Nagel's interview with Elliot Soloway satisfactorily address this issue? Cite examples from the texts to explain your response.

Chapter 2

1. Sue Shellenbarger claims that people who refuse to own smartphones prefer the simplicity and lower costs of feature phones. In your view, are these reasons compelling enough to not trade up to a smartphone? Why or why not?

2. Gerry Smith states that while smartphones make the Internet more accessible to low-income groups, they are not a replacement for computers and broadband services. In your opinion, do smartphones—despite their drawbacks— help close the digital divide? Provide examples from the viewpoint to support your answer.

Chapter 3

1. Timothy B. Lee warns that smartphone users face multiple risks to their privacy, from unknown surveillance to access of private data. Do you think Lee's privacy concerns are justified? Explain your reasoning.

2. Scott Thurm and Yukari Iwatani Kane assert that a *Wall Street Journal* investigation of 101 smartphone apps reveals numerous breaches of user privacy and profiling for marketing purposes. In your opinion, should the investigations' findings discourage the use of apps? Why or why not?

3. Scott Wright contends that lost and stolen smartphones pose a huge risk to personal and business privacy. Do you think Wright's concerns are justified? Cite examples from the viewpoint to support your reasoning.

Chapter 4

1. Barbara Hudson anticipates that the telecommunications industry will fail, leading to the obsolescence of the smartphone. Do you agree or disagree with Hudson? Explain your reasoning.

2. Charles Arthur argues that the smartphone will replace the personal computer (PC) with its portability, advanced capabilities, and affordability. Do you think Arthur provides a convincing prediction? Provide examples from the viewpoint to support your answer.

3. David W. Schropfer claims that users' preferences in the "format war" of the mobile wallet will decide what innovations will dominate and which will be lost. In your view, can the influence of consumers threaten the development of smartphone technologies? Why or why not?

Organizations to Contact

The editors have compiled the following list of organizations concerned with the issues debated in this book. The descriptions are derived from materials provided by the organizations. All have publications or information available for interested readers. The list was compiled on the date of publication of the present volume; the information provided here may change. Be aware that many organizations take several weeks or longer to respond to inquiries, so allow as much time as possible.

Center for Democracy & Technology (CDT)
1634 I Street NW, #1100, Washington, DC   20006
(202) 637-9800
website: www.cdt.org

The mission of the Center for Democracy & Technology (CDT) is to develop public policy solutions that advance constitutional civil liberties and democratic values in new computer and communications media. Pursuing its mission through policy research, public education, and coalition building, the center works to increase citizens' privacy and the public's control over the use of personal information held by government and other institutions. Its publications include issue briefs, policy papers, and *CDT Policy Posts*.

CTIA—The Wireless Association
1400 Sixteenth Street NW, Suite 600, Washington, DC   20036
(202) 736-3200 • fax: (202) 785-0721
website: www.ctia.org

CTIA—The Wireless Association is an international nonprofit membership organization that has represented the wireless communications industry since 1984. The association advocates on behalf of its members at all levels of government. CTIA also coordinates the industry's voluntary efforts to provide consumers with a variety of choices and information regarding their wireless products and services. This includes the voluntary industry guidelines, programs that promote mobile device recycling and reusing, and wireless accessibility for individuals with disabilities. The association offers a blog, e-mail news briefings, and a multimedia library on its website.

Electronic Frontier Foundation (EFF)
454 Shotwell Street, San Francisco, CA   94110-1914
(415) 436-9333 • fax: (415) 436-9993
e-mail: information@eff.org
website: www.eff.org

The Electronic Frontier Foundation (EFF) is an organization of students and other individuals that aims to promote a better understanding of telecommunications issues. It fosters awareness of civil liberties issues stemming from advancements in computer-based communications media and supports litigation to preserve, protect, and extend First Amendment rights in computing and telecommunications technologies. EFF's publications include the electronic newsletter *EFFector Online*, online bulletins, and reports.

Electronic Privacy Information Center (EPIC)
1718 Connecticut Avenue NW, Suite 200
Washington, DC   20009
(202) 483-1140 • fax: (202) 483-1248
website: www.epic.org

As an advocate of the public's right to electronic privacy, the Electronic Privacy Information Center (EPIC) sponsors educational and research programs, compiles statistics, and conducts litigation pertaining to privacy and other civil liberties. Its publications include the biweekly electronic newsletter *EPIC Alert* and reports such as "Smartphones and Election 2012."

Federal Trade Commission (FTC)
600 Pennsylvania Avenue NW, Washington, DC   20580
(202) 326-2222
website: www.ftc.gov

The Federal Trade Commission (FTC) deals with issues that touch the economic life of every American. It is the only federal agency with both consumer protection and competition jurisdiction in broad sectors of the economy. Its website offers information on mobile telecommunications, handheld devices, and smartphone applications, including issues relating to consumer privacy.

Mobile Marketing Association (MMA)
PO Box 3963, Bellevue, WA   98009-3963
(646) 257-4515
e-mail: mma@mmaglobal.com
website: www.mmaglobal.com

The Mobile Marketing Association (MMA) is a nonprofit trade association representing all players in the mobile marketing value chain. It works to promote, educate, measure, guide, and protect the mobile marketing industry worldwide. One of the association's objectives is to define and publish mobile marketing best practices and guidelines on privacy, ad delivery, and ad measurement. The association publishes a newsletter and the *International Journal of Mobile Marketing*.

Privacy International
46 Bedford Row, London   WC1R 4LR
  UK
+44 (0) 20 7242 2836
e-mail: info@privacy.org
website: www.privacyinternational.org

Privacy International is a nongovernmental organization with members in forty countries around the world. Its primary goal is to promote an international understanding of the importance of protecting individual privacy and personal data. Privacy International's website provides reports, studies, and commentary on current policy and technology issues, and also includes an online archive of information for students and researchers.

Privacy Rights Clearinghouse (PRC)
3108 Fifth Avenue, Suite A, San Diego, CA   92103
(619) 298-3396
website: www.privacyrights.org

The Privacy Rights Clearinghouse (PRC) is a nonprofit consumer organization with a two-part mission—to provide consumer information and advocate for consumer privacy. The group raises awareness of how technology affects personal privacy, empowers consumers to take action to control their own personal information by providing practical tips on privacy protection, responds to privacy-related complaints from consumers, and reports this information. Its website provides transcripts of PRC speeches and testimony, stories of consumer experiences, and numerous fact sheets, including "Hang Up on Harassment: Dealing with Cellular Phone Abuse" and "Privacy in the Age of the Smartphone."

Bibliography of Books

Ben Agger — *Oversharing: Presentations of Self in the Internet Age.* New York: Routledge, 2011.

Nancy K. Baym — *Personal Connections in the Digital Age.* Maiden, MA: Polity, 2010.

Nicholas Carr — *The Shallows: What the Internet Is Doing to Our Brains.* New York: W.W. Norton & Company, 2011.

Brian X. Chen — *Always On: How the iPhone Unlocked the Anything-Anytime-Anywhere Future—and Locked Us In.* Cambridge, MA: Da Capo Press, 2011.

Adriana de Souza e Silva and Jordan Frith — *Mobile Interfaces in Public Spaces: Locational Privacy, Control, and Urban Sociability.* New York: Routledge, 2012.

Anne Louise Gittleman — *Zapped: Why Your Cell Phone Shouldn't Be Your Alarm Clock and 1,268 Ways to Outsmart the Hazards of Electronic Pollution.* New York: HarperOne, 2010.

Eric Gordon and Adriana de Souza e Silva — *Net Locality: Why Location Matters in a Networked World.* Malden, MA: Wiley-Blackwell, 2011.

Chase Jarvis — *The Best Camera Is the One That's with You: iPhone Photography.* Berkeley, CA: New Riders, 2010.

Jeff Jarvis	*Public Parts: How Sharing in the Digital Age Improves the Way We Work and Live.* New York: Simon & Schuster, 2011.
Andrew Keen	*Digital Vertigo: How Today's Online Social Revolution Is Dividing, Diminishing, and Disorienting Us.* New York: St. Martin's Press, 2012.
Jaron Lanier	*You Are Not a Gadget: A Manifesto.* New York: Vintage Books, 2011.
Rich Ling	*New Tech, New Ties: How Mobile Communication Is Reshaping Social Cohesion.* Cambridge, MA: MIT Press, 2008.
Rich Ling and Scott W. Campbell, eds.	*Mobile Communication: Bringing Us Together and Tearing Us Apart.* New Brunswick, NJ: Transaction Publishers, 2011.
Chuck Martin	*The Third Screen: Marketing to Your Customers in a World Gone Mobile.* Boston, MA: Nicholas Brealey Publishing, 2011.
Susas Maushart	*The Winter of Our Disconnect: How Three Totally Wired Teenagers (and a Mother Who Slept with Her iPhone) Pulled the Plug on Their Technology and Lived to Tell the Tale.* New York: Jeremy P. Tarcher/Penguin, 2011.

James B. Murray Jr.
Wireless Nation: The Frenzied Launch of the Cellular Revolution in America. Cambridge, MA: Perseus Publishing, 2001.

Kevin D. Murray
Is My Cell Phone Bugged?: Everything You Need to Know to Keep Your Mobile Conversations Private. Austin, TX: Emerald Book Company, 2011.

John Palfrey and Urs Gasser
Born Digital: Understanding the First Generation of Digital Natives. New York: Basic Books, 2008.

Leslie A. Perlow
Sleeping with Your Smartphone: How to Break the 24/7 Habit and Change the Way You Work. Boston, MA: Harvard Business Review Press, 2012.

Larry D. Rosen
iDisorder: Understanding Our Obsession with Technology and Overcoming Its Hold on Us. New York: Palgrave Macmillan, 2012.

Michael Saylor
The Mobile Wave: How Mobile Intelligence Will Change Everything. New York: Vanguard Press, 2012.

Mark Shepard, ed.
Sentient City: Ubiquitous Computing, Architecture, and the Future of Urban Space. Cambridge, MA: MIT Press, 2011.

Pelle Snickars and Patrick Vonderau
Moving Data: The iPhone and the Future of Media. New York: Columbia University Press, 2012.

Sherry Turkle   *Alone Together: Why We Expect More from Technology and Less from Each Other.* New York: Basic Books, 2011.

Index

L

M